860.8
LAT   Latino voices

LATINO VOICES

LATINO VOICES

EDITED BY

FRANCES R. APARICIO

Writers of America

THE MILLBROOK PRESS
BROOKFIELD, CONNECTICUT

Library of Congress Cataloging-in-Publication Data
Latino voices / edited by Frances R. Aparicio.
p.   cm.—(Writers of America)
Summary: An anthology of Latino fiction, poetry, biography, and
other writings which describe the experiences of Hispanic Americans.
ISBN 1-56294-388-X (lib. bdg.)
1. Hispanic Americans—Literary collections.   [1. Hispanic
Americans—Literary collections.]   I. Aparicio, Frances R.
II. Series.
PZ5.L47   1994
860.8'098—dc20   93-42893   CIP   AC

Photographs courtesy of Bettmann Archive: p. 15; Impact
Visuals: pp. 26 (© Jeffrey Scott), 65 (© Donna Binder), 86 (©
Allan Clear); Sony Tropical: p. 39; Photo Researchers: p. 77
(© Vivienne della Grotta); UPI/Bettmann: p. 90; © Yolanda
Lopez: p. 99; © Frank Espada: p. 104; Liaison International:
p. 113 (© John Berry); © César Martínez: p. 116; © John
Valadez: p. 128.

Published by The Millbrook Press
2 Old New Milford Road, Brookfield, Connecticut 06804

Contents

LATINO VOICES

Introduction

WE LATINOS
AND LATINAS

Also known as Hispanics, Latinos and Latinas make up a fast-growing, dynamic, and diverse cultural group in the United States. The 1990 Census counted more than 22 million Latinos, mostly Mexican Americans, Puerto Ricans, and Cuban Americans. Since the early 1980s the largest group of Latinos coming to the United States has been the Central Americans, predominantly refugees who have fled the wartorn countries of Nicaragua and El Salvador. These immigrants have contributed yet other colorful segments to the already diverse mosaic that is Latino culture in the United States.

Latinos and Latinas come from the shores of the Caribbean islands of Cuba, Puerto Rico, and the Dominican Republic, from the volcanic mountains of Central America, from Mexico's arid north and the lush tropics of its central and southern regions. We come from large, modern Latin-American cities—Santiago, Caracas, Cartagena, and Bogotá, among others—as well as from small towns on the fringes of modernity. Many Latinos are born right here in the United States.

Some of our ancestors preceded the Pilgrims' arrival at Plymouth Rock. In the early sixteenth century, they began exploring and settling the southern, southwestern, and western regions of what is now the United States. Others— some in the southwestern United States and those in Puerto Rico—became American citizens as a result of invasion, war, and territorial occupation. Latinos have taken the oath of U.S. citizenship in New York City, having arrived by airplane with their entire lives packed into suitcases, or in Miami, having survived perilous sea journeys in rafts. Still others have crossed the U.S.-Mexico border illegally and have found work when and where they could.

Latinos are not a race but a mixture of European, African, and Indian peoples. We are *mestizos* and *mulattos*—blends of European with Indian and African. We are blond, blue-eyed, and of German, Russian, French, and English ancestry. And we wear proudly the dark skin of our Indian or African heritage.

We are Catholic, Jewish, Muslim, Pentecostal, and Mormon, among many other religions.

We speak Spanish, but very different oral versions of it, using diverse words for the same things. Many Latinos born in the United States speak only English.

Although we have been labeled Hispanic by the U.S. government, usually for statistical purposes, most of us still identify ourselves with our national group—as Puerto Ricans, Mexicans, Chileans, or Nicaraguans, for example. We defy labels, though the terms *Latino* and *Latina,* while imperfect, are preferable to *Hispanic,* which erases our multiple ethnic heritages.

We have been altogether too much erased from U.S. history. Textbooks have ignored the hundreds of years of our presence and contributions to this society. Through the gains made during the Civil Rights Movement and one of its Latino equivalents, the Chicano Movement, during the 1960s, what we have brought from our differing legacies and given to the United States is now being recognized and integrated into the books that you and I read.

Latinos themselves have also attempted to wipe away their own pasts. Because we have been colonized in our native lands and subjected to prejudice here in the United States, we have suppressed our identities. Being colonized has meant that a foreign government, the United States, has taken away our land, defined our laws, and robbed us of our self-determination. In Puerto Rico, young men can be drafted into the U.S. Army but remain without the right to choose the president who would declare war. This has made us ashamed of who we are, as has ridicule of our names, language, and customs on the mainland. Many Latinos have grown up rejecting themselves, ignoring their history.

Latinos have transcended both colonization and prejudice, however. We have fitted into American society, taking high seats in business and government. And we have remained stubbornly on its fringes, refusing to be assimilated. From this bicultural point of view, from the *frontera*, or border, of living both between and in two worlds, we—and especially our Latino and Latina writers—have forged a new vision of the United States.

I invite you to share that vision in the pages that follow. The writers you are about to read, the Latino and Latina voices you are about to hear, call out with news from an astonishing variety of places and times. Rafael Chacón writes of how his fellow Mexicans reacted when the U.S. Army invaded their home in the Southwest in 1846. Judith

Ortiz Cofer depicts women in traditional Puerto Rican families exercising at home the authority and independence they surrendered to their husbands and fathers in the outside world.

These writers' means of communication are as diverse as their messages. In addition to personal, true-life narratives, you will encounter the vibrant poetry of Victor Hernández Cruz and the witty fiction of Sandra Cisneros.

What these Latino and Latina voices have to say—and the ways in which they say it—are indivisible from the larger story of this nation. Thus, they truly belong to writers of America.

Frances R. Aparicio
Associate Professor of Romance Languages
and Literatures and American Culture
The University of Michigan, Ann Arbor

COMING TO THE U.S., AND THE U.S. COMING TO US

IN THE BEGINNING

The story of Latinos in the United States began, for many, not with coming to the United States but with the United States coming to them. During the first half of the 1800s, what are today the states of California, New Mexico, Arizona, Texas, and Colorado were part of a region belonging to Mexico: the Rio Grande valley.

In 1821, William Becknell, a trader from the fledgling United States, opened the Santa Fe Trail. The trail established a trade route between the United States and the entire Rio Grande valley region. Within twenty-five years, a trickle of traders, trappers, and settlers from the United States turned into a flood.

Other American newcomers to the region rode on the crest of a wave called Manifest Destiny. Manifest Destiny, a term coined in 1845, described a belief held by many in the United States that the nation had the right—and indeed the duty—to rule the land between the Atlantic and Pacific oceans. That meant taking over Mexican land. The enforcers of this belief were U.S. troops. The troops clashed with the Mexican Army, and the Mexican-American War began in 1846. Trapped in the middle were Mexican civilians and Indians.

RAFAEL CHACÓN

Rafael Chacón, a Mexican living in what is now New Mexico, was thirteen when U.S. troops arrived in Taos in 1846. In his autobiography, Legacy of Honor, *he wrote of how his introduction to the United States came not from immigration but from invasion.*

I remember that there was such terror instilled by the Americans that when a dog barked the people killed it, the burros were muzzled so they could not bray, and if the roosters crowed at daylight they killed them. Only at night were fires permitted in order that the enemy could not discover the smoke from the huts. After the assault on the *pueblo* of Taos, where the Indians fought with much vigor, the Americans seized some Indians and Mexicans and executed them, after which all was peaceful once more. As soon as they considered the countryside conquered, they sent some companies of soldiers to Mexico. The people fled in terror and the soldiers burned the public markets, the granaries, and everything the people were not able to carry away. My father's brother, Don Damacio Chacón, was without even mattresses for his family to use but, being an industrious and hardworking man, in six months already had his house rebuilt and refurnished.

pueblo—people or village

General Winfield Scott leads U.S. forces into Mexico City during the Mexican-American War. They captured the city, ended the war, and land belonging to Mexico was taken over by the United States.

FIRST IMPRESSIONS

While Mexicans and Mexican Americans had been living in North America and the United States since the sixteenth century, other Latinos began immigrating to the U.S. during the nineteenth century. They came from Cuba fleeing oppression under Spain. They came from the sugarcane fields of Puerto Rico seeking opportunity. They came from Mexico and Central and Latin America. Each group had its own expectations for the future—and memories of the past—and brought with it its own unique culture.

No matter when they came or from where, however, most were united by a sensation of utter strangeness when they first laid eyes on their new homes. They were surprised, repulsed, and enchanted—sometimes all at once.

VICTOR HERNÁNDEZ CRUZ

Poet Victor Hernández Cruz was born in Aguas Buenas, Puerto Rico, in 1949 and immigrated to New York City with his family as a young boy. He published his first book of poetry, Snaps, *the year he turned nineteen.*

He recalls his first impressions of New York in the 1950s in this poem, "Snaps of Immigration," from his collection Red Beans.

1
I remember the fragrance of
the Caribbean
A scent that anchors into the
ports of technology.

2
I dream with suitcases
full of illegal fruits
Interned between white
guayaberas that dissolved
Into snowflaked polyester.

3
When we saw the tenements
our eyes turned backwards

to the miracle of scenery
At the supermarket
My mother caressed the
Parsley.

4
We came in the middle of winter
from another time
We took a trip into the future
A fragment of another planet
To a place where time flew
As if clocks had coconut oil
put on them.

5
Rural mountain dirt walk
Had to be adjusted to cement
pavement
The new city finished the
concrete supply of the world
Even the sky was cement
The streets were made of shit.

6
The past was dissolving like
sugar at the bottom of a coffee cup
That small piece of earth that
we habitated
Was somewhere in a television
Waving in space.

7
From beneath the ice
From beneath the cement

From beneath the tar
From beneath the pipes and wires
Came the cucurucu of the roosters.

8
People wrote letters as if they
were writing the scriptures
Penmanship of women who made
tapestry with their hands
Cooked *criollo* pots
Fashioned words of hope and longing
Men made ink out of love
And saw their sweethearts
Wearing yellow dresses
Reaching from the balcony
To the hands of the mailman.

9
At first English was nothing
but sound
Like trumpets doing yakity yak
As we found meanings for the words
We noticed that many times the
Letters deceived the sound
What could we do
It was the language of a
foreign land.

criollo—Creole; combining European and Latin American
     qualities
guayaberas—men's shirts that are quite popular in the Ca-
     ribbean

STICKING OUT, FITTING IN

For many Latinos the sensation of strangeness lingered long after their first impressions. It became part of their identities. Some chose to accept this perpetual feeling of being out of place. Others struggled to erase all traces of their origins: They dressed "American," acted "American," and—though they were often betrayed by their tongues, trained in another language—tried to sound "American."

JULIA ALVAREZ

The speaker of this excerpt from the novel How the Garcia Girls Lost Their Accents *celebrates her difference. She finds it reflected in the world around her—even in the very climate. The novel is set in the early 1960s, when tensions between the United States and the Communist governments of the Soviet Union and Cuba ran high. The author, Julia Alvarez, is a poet and writer from the Dominican Republic.*

Our first year in New York we rented a small apartment with a Catholic school nearby, taught by the Sisters of Charity, hefty women in long black gowns and bonnets that made them look peculiar, like dolls in mourning. I liked them a lot, especially my grandmotherly fourth-grade teacher, Sister Zoe. I had a lovely name, she said, and she had me teach the whole class how to pronounce it. *Yo-lan-da.* As the only immigrant in my class, I was put in a special seat in the first row by the window, apart from the other children so that Sister Zoe could tutor me without disturbing them. Slowly, she enunciated the new words I was to repeat: *laundromat, corn flakes, subway, snow.*

Soon I picked up enough English to understand holocaust was in the air. Sister Zoe explained to a wide-eyed classroom what was happening in Cuba. Russian missiles were being assembled, trained supposedly on New York City. President Kennedy, looking worried too, was on the television at home, explaining we might have to go to war against the Communists. At school, we had air-raid drills: an ominous bell would go off and we'd file into the hall, fall to the floor, cover our heads with our coats, and imagine our hair falling out, the bones in our arms going soft. At home, Mami and my sisters and I said a rosary for world peace. I heard new vocabulary: *nuclear bomb, radioactive fallout, bomb shelter.* Sister Zoe explained how it would happen. She drew a picture of a mushroom on the blackboard and dotted a flurry of chalk marks for the dusty fallout that would kill us all.

The months grew cold, November, December. It was dark when I got up in the morning, frosty when I followed my breath to school. One morning as I sat at my desk daydreaming out the window, I saw dots in the air like the ones Sister Zoe had drawn—random at first, then lots and lots. I shrieked, "Bomb! Bomb!" Sister Zoe jerked around, her full black skirt ballooning as she hurried to my side. A few girls began to cry.

But then Sister Zoe's shocked look faded. "Why, Yolanda dear, that's snow!" She laughed. "Snow."

"Snow," I repeated. I looked out the window warily. All my life I had heard about the white crystals that fell out of American skies in the winter. From my desk I watched the fine powder dust the sidewalk and parked cars below. Each flake was different, Sister Zoe had said, like a person, irreplaceable and beautiful.

DAVID UNGER

For others, the sense of difference became unbearable. But if sticking out was painful, struggling to fit in was equally so. Writer and translator David Unger was born in Guatemala in 1950. He came to the United States at age four. This excerpt is from his essay "Roots: A Crosscultural Context."

My parents chose to settle in Florida, a five-hour propeller flight from the family in Guatemala. Miami at the time was a backwoods place, dull as can be, and the heat—before air-conditioning became standard—was overwhelming. We became part of the Anglo world, in those days made up—at least in Hialeah—of Southerners, racist to the core, who had left Georgia or northern Florida in search of work, many of them finding employment as airline mechanics in the fledgling Miami International Airport. In one fell swoop, I abandoned my Spanish, forgot the mountains, lakes and volcanoes of my homeland, and obliterated from memory the *roscas, espumillas,* and *canillas de leche* that my parents bought us as treats. We were in the land of *Mae and Dave's Hot Dogs and Hamburgers.* Ketchup on everything. This provoked an identity crisis in me: Who am I? I pondered, lying in bed, trying not to move for fear of kindling the wrath of Sweat, the Goddess of Heat.

We were different, no two ways about it. I never confided this to my parents, but I figured I differed from my classmates in three ways: I was Guatemalan, Jewish, and left-handed. No one could claim that. My childhood hero became Sandy Koufax, the hard-throwing southpaw of the Los Angeles Dodgers, who missed his starting assignment in the 1959 World Series to commemorate Yom Kippur, the Jewish Day of Atonement. Being left-handed screwed up my penmanship—my drawings were pitiful—but as a ball-player, it meant I could probably eke out a walk. Being Jewish led to fistfights and bloody noses as I defended the ancestral roots I knew little about and which, to my opponents, was simply a word batted around by their anti-Semitic parents. How strange it was when Bubba Phillips called me a *spic* and I—without knowing what the word meant—got him into a hammer-head lock until he took it back. In those days I was so confused that I even got into a fight when someone called me a *kraut*.

So what was this Guatemala thing? Was it a word to jot down whenever I was asked to note my place of birth? It became the awkwardness that made me pronounce *think* as *tink* and forced me to write dozens of social studies reports about this pitcher-shaped country in Central America which, like a shooting star, was quickly receding from memory. And that last name Unger, quickly transformed to the *Ungawa* of Tarzan films—Swahili for elephant poop, so said my friends—why couldn't it be more recognizably Latin like Ramírez or Sánchez? With no answers, I took the road of least resistance, forced myself, albeit unconsciously, to forget as much Spanish as I could. When I was eight, making my first trip back to visit relatives in Guatemala, I barely knew 300 words of Spanish. *Buenos días*, if I was forced to speak, or maybe something like *tengo hambre* or *necesito hacer pipí*. So much for roots.

buenos días—good day
canillas de leche—milk-based candies
espumillas—meringue
necesito hacer pipí—I have to pee
roscas—twist-shaped pastries
tengo hambre—I'm hungry

THE END OF THE ROAD

Whether they stick out or fit in, most Latinos come to the United States expecting a new beginning. This is not so for Mexicans who enter the country illegally. Insultingly called *wetbacks* or *wets*, these men and women are often stopped by U.S. border police, known as *La Migra*. Their first moments in the new land quickly become their last as they are sent back to Mexico—often to attempt to cross again.

RAMÓN "TIANGUIS" PÉREZ

In "La Migra," an excerpt from his book Diary of an Undocumented Immigrant, *Mexican-American writer Ramón "Tianguis" Pérez describes the danger that illegal immigrants risk in coming to the United States. He also portrays the frustration of coming to a new land only to find it is the end of the road.*

On the fifth day they make preparations for the trip. Because the preacher, Juan and I are the shortest, they put us in the trunk of the car: the preacher, Juan and me. Six more go in the seats. As soon as the driver has us loaded, he takes off.

We turn several corners on the streets of town. Then we feel the car pick up speed and that makes us think that we're on a freeway. I am on one side of the trunk, the preacher is in the middle, and Juan is on the other side. The floor of the trunk is lacking the carpet that it probably once had, and it's not very comfortable riding upon a sheet of pressed steel. Just above my head are vents that allow me to see the clear sky. It is deep blue. The vents were apparently created, or left in the car when its rear sound speakers were removed.

At least, through them I'm able to breathe air that isn't as hot as the air from the trunk. Besides giving me air and a view of the sky, the vents let me see up into the rear windshield, which is big enough and curved enough to work as a kind of periscope. I can see reflections in it of the four guys in the back seat, and of the two who are riding next to the driver who is smoking. I can even glimpse at the road ahead.

"I hope we arrive," Juan says.

"God willing," the preacher responds.

I tell them about the panorama I can see, but they don't take heart. "From here I can see when the *Migra* shows," I tell them, to ease the tension that has overtaken us.

They don't take kindly to my remark. "Shut up, man. Don't even think about that," the preacher says.

After about half an hour, the trunk is uncomfortably hot. Because I'm close to the tire, it's completely impossible for me to stay still. The sheet steel beneath me little by little grows hotter until I have to change positions. I feel like a roasting chicken and I don't want to imagine how much hotter it could become. I inform the other two and Juan hands me his jacket. I wad it up and put it between my back and the steel and it gives me some relief.

We make some quick comments about those who are riding in the seats, and conclude that they aren't as comfortable as might seem.

"Right now," Juan says, "some of them probably have numb legs."

"Accidents happen all the time," the preacher says, "and we're neither the first nor the last to travel in a trunk."

Such comments are nothing more than a manner of infusing ourselves with confidence, because anecdotes always come to mind. In the house of Juan Serna, a wet told us that he'd seen three others fried like bacon in a trunk. The tragedy happened when the car in which they were riding caught fire. The driver, foreseeing that the police would come, took flight and perhaps without thinking, took the keys with him. There was no way to get the men out who were in the trunk. I look at the preacher to see what spirits he's in, and I see that his eyes are closed and his lips are moving rapidly, as if he's in prayer.

The car makes some turns. We leave the pavement, go onto a dirt road, and just as quickly return to pavement again. We know this because on pavement the rattling stops and on dirt roads, the bumping and noise starts up again, throwing us about like dice in a gambler's hand. Some little holes in the floor of the trunk let dust in, and little by little, a cloud of dust forms in our space. Juan puts a handkerchief over his nose and the preacher fans the air with his hands in vain.

"All of this to get to Houston," the preacher says.

"When we get there, we're really going to need a bath," Juan comments.

From my observatory I see passing scenes of land covered with dry, yellow grass, and every few seconds, lines of barbed wire pass before my view. Sometimes I see a thing or two that's further off.

About two hours later, the driver utters a profanity that Jesus himself may have heard, and that probably offended the Virgin. With the fist of his right hand he beats upon the steering wheel. He brakes sharply, shaking us, and the tires of the car skid in the dirt. "Run!" we hear him shout, and immediately we hear the doors opening. Those of us in the trunk know that the trip has been frustrated, but we don't want to believe it.

The rearview mirror of a Migra *patrol car shows a Mexican crossing into the United States via a hole in a border fence. He is likely to be captured, detained, and returned home—to make many more attempts at coming to America.*

The sound of a car comes closer and it brakes next to us. I can see it clearly in the reflections of the windshield. It's a light green car, a *Migra* patrol car, but I don't tell my companions this because they will see it soon enough, and I don't want to be the bird who brings bad news.

We hear the sound of the car's door opening and closing.

"Why are you running, you idiot!" we hear somebody shout in badly pronounced Spanish. Inside the car, only one of our companions is left.

We hear slow and heavy steps close to our car, then the sound of a key being placed in the lock. Above us, a blond Anglo holds open the door of the trunk. He's tall and bald, and wearing a dark green uniform. A pipe rests between his lips.

He smiles in a joking and friendly way.

"How comfortable you are," he says wryly. "Get out."

When the three of us are outside, he tells us to sit on the tail of the car without closing the trunk. The rest of our companions are lined up against the side of the car with the exception of one, who is climbing a barbed wire fence, on his way back. He must have been the one to whom the word "idiot" was addressed. Looking at the terrain behind us, it's clear that escape is impossible. The land is a plain of dried grass and its few bushes don't even have leaves. We captives lament what's happened by exchanging glances and making gestures with our heads. But then I notice that the driver is missing.

The agent comes and goes in front of us, unhurried and unworried. He takes long, heavy steps and looks us over closely, as if we were exhibiting ourselves.

"Which one of you is the driver?" he suddenly asks.

"None of us," three voices answer.

The agent goes over to his car, takes out a walkie-talkie, speaks with someone, and then comes back. He is smiling triumphantly.

"Where did you think you were going?" he asks.

"To Houston," one of us says.

Then he asks how much we were to pay. "Why did you decide to come now?" he says, enjoying himself. "Why couldn't you wait until tomorrow? That's my day off!"

"Let us go," Juan says.

The agent laughs.

"No, that's not possible," he says, still in high spirits. "You guys ought to go back to Mexico and find a smarter coyote."

"Are all of you Mexicans?" he asks, scrutinizing us. "You're Salvadoran," he suddenly says, pointing to the preacher.

"I am Mexican," the preacher serenely answers. "I'm more Mexican than *Emiliano Zapata* [the Mexican revolutionary]."

After a long silence the agent says, "If you are carrying a pistol, knife, cocaine or marijuana, take it out and hand it over."

Nobody answers.

"At last," the agent says, perhaps just to break the silence, "are you going to tell me who the driver is?"

A few minutes later two Border Patrol vehicles pull up. One is like the car that showed up first, the other is a van, one of those that we wetbacks know as *perreras*, or dog wagons.

The agent who stopped us points in the direction in which the driver escaped. His companions make use of their radios. They order us to get into the *perrera*, where we encounter eight other wets. The windows of the *perrera* are covered with heavy metal screens.

A half hour later, we find ourselves in the Immigration offices in the little south Texas town of Hebbronville; they consist of three one-story buildings arranged in the form of a U on one side of a highway. The middle of the U is a paved parking lot where three more patrol vehicles are stationed. Nine of us are locked in a cell in one of the buildings. Inside the building are ten agents, most of them Mexican Americans, who go back and forth from outside into the office. A couple of them sit in chairs behind desks.

A bronze-skinned agent with a sparse moustache comes up to our cell and recites the following words: "You are detained for having illegally entered the country. We are going to investigate you, but first you must know your rights. You can refuse to answer our questions and you can request the presence of an attorney, and if you don't have one, we'll provide one."

None of us asks for an attorney.

Our cell has three concrete walls, and the side that looks out onto the office is covered by a wire screen. Inside the cell are urinals, a sink and concrete benches. A few minutes pass before they call us, one by one, to make our statements.

The questions: How many times have you been detained by Immigration agents? Have you ever been arrested by the police? Where were you born? What are the names of your parents? Where do you come from?

The agent who questions me also writes down my physical description. He hands me the form with my answers written upon it, gives me a pen, and points to the spot where I should sign, beneath a paragraph saying that I voluntarily leave the country for having infringed upon its laws.

When I walk back towards the cell, I discover that they've also detained the driver. He's short and skinny. His slightly oval face is stained by sweat that has dried, and grains of sand seem to have impregnated his pores. They have him handcuffed in a cell two doors down from us. He's seated in a chair and his slumped body gives the impression that at any minute, he might fall down. His eyes are deeply sad, melancholy. His condition makes me feel sorry for him. He is the image of a condemned man.

Upon seeing me his eyes dart left and right, and seeing that none of the agents is looking, to my surprise he lets his face adopt a look of absolute tranquility, as if in possession of himself. He makes a sign, raising his right index finger to his lips, even though to do it he has to move both hands because he's cuffed. He tells me not to say anything about him. I move my head a little to show him that they haven't asked me about him. He seems convinced. To my admiration, he then returns to looking sad. He should have been an actor in the theatre.

When they've interrogated all of us, they call us in alphabetical order towards the door where an agent hands us a copy of the paper we've signed. Another agent is waiting for us at the door of the *perrera.*

"And this?" Juan asks when they hand him his paper. "Is this our passport?"

"Yeah, sure it is. It's the passport to your country," an agent says, savoring Juan's quip.

In less than half an hour they discharge us at the entrance to the international bridge in Laredo. Each one of us pays ten American cents and we walk in silence over the bridge.

Meanwhile, I try to gather my thoughts, to decide if I should cross again or not. I've run into complications now for more than two weeks, and I can't imagine that a new attempt would be any easier. The possibility of returning home turns around in my head, but I also think that I already owe a sum of dollars, and I'm now at the border.

"What are you going to do, Juan?" I ask, because he's the most experienced among us.

He turns towards me, looking at my shoulders with his tired eyes and with an air of certainty he says, "Well, what else? Cross again!"

OUR HOMES

Where Latinos and Latinas have lived in the United States has influenced their cultural expressions—the music, art, and, especially, the literature they create.

ANCESTRAL LAND

Many Mexican Americans call the rural Southwest Aztlán, a name that calls to mind a mythic ancestral land. The Mexican culture of this region has always been deeply rooted in oral traditions and folklore. In 1848, Mexico signed the Guadalupe Hidalgo treaty ending the Mexican-American War and ceding large portions of Aztlán to the United States. Since then, many families have been moved and removed from their homes to make way for mining companies, railroads, cities, and the approaching U.S. culture. During times of transition, people have told the tales and legends of their ancestors for a sense of continuity with the past. Yet these stories have also changed to reflect the new circumstances of their telling.

32

MARGARITA MARTÍNEZ

Margarita Martínez was born in 1890 on a ranch called Los Reales (The Royal Ones) near Tucson, Arizona. She recounts the hardships that people endured in her early days, the changes that came with the approach of U.S. culture, and she speaks of the impact that the Mexican legend of La Llorona *had on her. This story is part of a collection of testimonies by Mexican elders in Arizona called* Images and Conversations.

My grandmother was here when the first train arrived. She used to wash for the families of the men who worked for the railroad—laying the track. Those families were poor, but not as poor as the rest of us, because they had regular paying jobs. After the day's work was done, my grandmother would say to me, "*Vámonos, mijita. Vamos a llevar la ropa.*" ("Come on, my little daughter. We shall go and deliver the clothes.")

And she would tie up the day's wash in a bundle and we would take the bundle with the clean clothing and deliver it to the families. On the way, we would pass the flour mill. The flour mill had doors above and a scale below. That's where they would put the sacks of wheat to weigh them. They grew wheat along the river in those days. Some people would buy large amounts, and some people would buy small amounts. We would always buy a little sack of wheat for the hens and the little chicks. We always had fresh eggs, and I was used to that. But then the Americans came, and I guess they don't like chickens because they always buy their eggs in a box.

There was in the old days a little house along the river. It was before you get to Callejón Carrillo. They used to say that the man and woman and their children who used to live there used to make adobes to sell. They had a little well and they used to haul their water out with a wheel and pulley and rope. Of course, when I was little, the house was no longer there—there was nothing left of the well or the pulley. And the ladies who used to wash at the river used to say, "*Vámonos temprano, antes de que se aparezca el espanto.*" ("Let's go home early, before the ghost appears.") As soon as it gets dark, you will be able to see a woman's ghost. She is taking water out of the well and then you can hear pulleys squeak and make noise. And they could hear the water sloshing around in the bucket. And everyone was very much afraid.

I remember the old Mission Church of San Cosme. There were a few ruins left—huge stones and adobes. There was a small room that was still standing. I remember how it looked—it had only one entrance. People used to say that there was buried treasure there. There was a woman who had divining rods which she used to look for the gold. She would hire out men so that they could dig for the treasure in those rooms. My husband didn't care to join in the search. He used to say, "When you're poor, you're poor, and when you're rich, you're rich. Don't look for that which you have not lost."

The little house that my husband and I built still stands. It is on Melwood Street. My son still lives there. We had a little *milpa* there—not far from the river, and we used to plant with the will of God. When the season for planting was over, my husband would go and work in the dairy. That way we would have money for food and other necessities until the harvest. We would plant beans and corn and squash and watermelon. We have a picture of one of the pumpkins that we grew on our little *milpa*—it was huge. Later, when the railroad came through, they bought that little piece of land that we had.

You know, when I was young, we were very innocent and simple—not like the young people of today. We used to believe everything. An old man, the brother of my father-in-law, told us that story of *La Llorona*. I never heard her or saw her, but I used to use the story to make my children behave when they wouldn't go to sleep at night. I used to tell them, "Quiet down, or La Llorona will come and get you." Anyway, the old man said that La Llorona had been a wicked girl. She would have *babitos* (little babies) and she didn't know what to do with them. And so she would throw them in the river and drown them. She had already had seven children when she died. And *Tatadios* would not let her into heaven. He made her return to earth and gather her children out of the river, because that's where she had drowned them. And she cannot go to heaven until she finds all her children. And that is why she cries and wails—because she is looking for her children, and she cannot go to heaven until she finds all her children. I don't believe that it is her real body that is wandering; I believe it must be her soul—her spirit. And when the Santa Cruz River floods, that's when she is supposed to cry.

La Llorona—the Wailing Woman, a legendary Mexican figure
milpa—cornfield
Tatadios—God the Father; *Tata* is an Indian term in Mexico used to address one's father or grandfather

THE BARRIO

Since the turn of the century, New York City has been the port of entry for most Puerto Ricans coming to the United States. They have established themselves in *barrios*, or working-class ethnic neighborhoods, where their language and culture flourished. In the early 1990s, New York City was home to almost two million Puerto Ricans, and to fast-growing communities of Dominicans and Colombians.

Many young Latinos and Latinas have survived not only the rampant poverty and the conditions of neglect that surround them, but also prevailing Anglo stereotypes of Latino violence, and abuse of drugs and welfare. The cultural vitality of Latinos in the cities cannot be ignored. Their food, language, murals, religious iconography, and popular music have traveled out of the barrios, transforming U.S. culture and achieving international fame.

WILLIE COLÓN

The following piece, entitled "The Rhythms," was written by Willie Colón, one of the most famous Latino composers and trombonists in the United States and Latin America. Born in 1950, Colón recorded his first album at age fifteen. He has since been nominated for Grammy Awards and has performed all over the world.

This Puerto Rican musician from the Bronx shares his own memories of growing up in the barrio, as he describes how important Afro-Caribbean rhythms and music have been in helping Latinos to maintain a sense of self and cultural identity amid the poverty and the racism that they encounter. Today Latin music has permeated all levels of media and popular culture here and abroad.

ᕮᐸᕽ 139th Street in the South Bronx in the late 50's and early 60's was no longer a part of the United States, much to the chagrin of the Italian and Irish working-class population who would come down with serious cases of "White Flight" anytime more than six of us moved in.

We easily turned 139th Street into a tropical *barriada*. All the stores in the area had Spanish signs in front. In the mornings you could hear the radios blaring those Latin rhythms in an eerie but reassuring echoey unison—and the smell of hundreds of pots of Cafe Bustelo filling the air.

Abuela came to live with us when Felix [her husband] died of undetermined causes. (*Abuela* said it had to be because of that damned motorcycle he had. He used to ride *Abuela* around town in a sidecar.)

She used to look at me with glazed eyes: you see, psychologically to her, I think, I was Gilberto [her son who died at age seven], reborn. She would tell me that Gilberto was my guardian angel and was always with me. But I needed an instrument to play. Yeah, she pushed the rhythm on me.

But the rhythm was very important to all of us. On 139th Street it would be my lullaby. Conga drums and chants echoing through the streets and alleyways in the late afternoon. I would lie in bed with my bottle (baby bottle) and listen to the *coros* as I watched the light from the headlights of the cars that would come down the hill track across the wall of my bedroom.

Occasionally, someone would start banging a bottle or tin can. He would usually stop soon afterwards either from fatigue or by popular demand if he fell out of time. . . . "Don't come around messing up our jam, Bro!"

The night had . . . rhythm.

So much so that when the music outside stopped, we'd say "What the Hell was that!" There was something wrong. Like in those old Tarzan movies when he'd stop and notice that the drums stopped. That made a lot of sense to me.

Soon after, our rhythmic security force would start up again and we could all go back to sleep.

The rhythms protected us. . . .

In the 40's, the rhythm was the rage. The upper class *conga*ed and *samba*ed and *rhumba*ed at every movie gangster's posh *bougie* supper club. Lucille Ball and Desi Arnaz brought the rhythm into the American living room in the 50's.

Now we had our foot in the door; Pepino (Cucumber) from "The Real McCoys" and Ricky, Mr. Babaloo.

The rhythms gave us . . . faces.

The 60's was the Roots generation. We saw the emergence of Black Power, Weathermen, Radicals, Anti-War Activists, Flower Power, The Young Lords (with Felipe Luciano and Pablo Yoruba Guzman) and the Flower Children.

Meanwhile, back on 139th Street, I was starting my first band, the Dandees. My mom dyed some shirts pink for us and printed "The Dandees" on the back with a Magic Marker. It was a quartet: a conga, an accordion, a clarinet, and me on the trumpet that *Abuela* had bought from the pawn shop for $50. I was on my way!

The Beatles, The Animals and Paul Revere and the Raiders were burning up the charts. But I was playing *bombas* and *plenas, son montunos,* and *merengues.* I recorded my first LP in 1967.

I was discovered at one of the dances that were the new thing. Most of the Hispanic and some black teens were learning how to "Latin."

Willie Colon, the king of salsa, *plays before the flag of Puerto Rico. A fusion of many Latino musical styles, salsa was born in the* barrio, *but has moved far beyond its boundaries and symbolizes the cultural exchange between Latinos and other Americans.*

Clubs like the Cheetah, Colgate Gardens, La Mancha, Casino 14, the Hotel St. George and Chez José were constantly filled to capacity. Thousands of teens getting into the rhythms three or four nights a week!

Our generation was mostly U.S.-born, so when I started a song with a Puerto Rican *aguinaldo* that went into a Cuban *son montuno* and then into a Dominican *merengue*, with occasional English or Spanglish choruses, nobody flinched . . . except for some of the old-timers who nearly had apoplexy. It was blasphemous! It was incorrect! It was . . . *salsa!*

From the late 60's thru the 70's *salsa* was international: not only in New York, where it started, but in Panama, Venezuela, Santo Domingo, Peru, Colombia, Mexico. Madison Square Garden, The Cow Palace, Yankee Stadium, Hiram Bithorn Stadium, The Hollywood Paladium. We traveled to Tokyo, Paris, Cannes, Zaire! Santana's *Black Magic Woman* and *Oye Como Va* were No. 1.

The rhythms brought us together. . . .

Today we hear Frank Sinatra, Miami Sound Machine, Paul Simon, Debarge, Shelia E., Madonna, Yes, Prince, Herb Albert, and almost every pop and rock group has the rhythm on their record tracks and performances.

Listen to the commercial background music; some of it is even way up front like the Citrus Hill orange juice and the "Wouldn't you rather have a Buick" commercials.

The other day I was playing Television Roulette when I stopped on the Nashville Station, Channel 30. There was a Blue Grass group with long beards and all, and in the back was an 350-lb. fella wearing coveralls and banging away on a pair of conga drums. I said to myself, "That's it . . . now I've seen everything!"

The rhythm has become part of the "Heartbeat of America."

Abuela—Grandmother
aguinaldo—traditional Christmas song from Puerto Rico
barriada—ethnic enclave, neighborhood

bomba—a Puerto Rican dance that originated in the sugarcane plantations among the African slaves

bougie—a Latin dance based on the boogaloo of the early
1960s

conga—an Afro-Cuban dance

coros—choruses

merengue—a popular dance from the Dominican Republic

plenas—an Afro-Puerto Rican dance and music; the songs
narrate events from the point of view of the working class

rhumba—an Afro-Cuban dance and music

salsa—Latin popular music that emerged in New York during the early 1960s; it synthesizes diverse Afro-Cuban and
Afro-Puerto Rican musical forms mentioned above

samba—a popular Afro-Brazilian dance and music

son montuno—Afro-Cuban rhythm

THE 'BURBS

For upper- and middle-class Latino families, life in the suburbs represents the fulfillment of the American Dream. The
desire to own a home, two cars, and have their children in
good schools and in a less troubled environment has moti-
vated Latinos to escape the problems of urban life and to
settle down in the suburbs.

Yet this "ideal" environment has not always proven to be
a haven for Latinos and other minorities. They encounter the
brick wall of prejudice, residential segregation, negative
stereotypes, and ridicule of their language as part and parcel
of middle- and upper-class communities. Thus, many Latinos end up isolated or else meld into the homogeneous
lifestyle of American suburbia, losing their ethnic identity.

PIRI THOMAS

Piri Thomas is a black Puerto Rican author who first ex-
posed the racial violence, drug abuse, and gang culture in
Spanish Harlem in his classic novel Down These Mean
Streets *(1967). Piri Thomas was born in New York City in*
1928 and grew up in Spanish Harlem during the Depression
years. While serving six years in prison for armed robbery,
he began his rehabilitation. Since then, he has been develop-
ing rehabilitation programs and lecturing across the coun-
try and at universities. The following piece, entitled
"Babylon for the Babylonians," narrates what Thomas, the
author-protagonist, encounters in the suburbs of Long Is-
land, the home long desired by his parents.

In 1944 we moved to Long Island. Poppa was making
good money at the airplane factory, and he had saved
enough bread for a down payment on a small house.

As we got our belongings ready for the moving van, I
stood by watching all the hustling with a mean feeling. My
hands weren't with it; my fingers played with the top of a
cardboard box full of dishes. My face tried hard not to show
resentment at Poppa's decision to leave my streets forever. I
felt that I belonged in Harlem; it was my kind of kick. I didn't
want to move out to Long Island. My friend Crutch had told
me there were a lot of paddies out there, and they didn't dig
Negroes or Puerto Ricans.

"Piri," Momma said.

"Yeah, Moms." I looked up at Momma. She seemed tired
and beat. Still thinking about Paulie all the time and how she
took him to the hospital just to get some simple-assed tonsils
out. And Paulie died. I remember she used to keep repeat-
ing how Paulie kept crying, "Don't leave me, Mommie," and

her saying, "Don't worry, *nene*, it's just for a day." Paulie—I pushed his name out of my mind.

"*Dios mío*, help a little, *hijo*," Momma said.

"Moms, why do we gotta move outta Harlem? We don't know any other place better'n this."

"*Caramba!* What ideas," Momma said. "What for you talk like that? Your Poppa and I saved enough money. We want you kids to have good opportunities. It is a better life in the country. No like Puerto Rico, but it have trees and grass and nice schools."

"Yeah, Moms. Have they got Puerto Ricans out there?"

"*Sí*, I'm sure. Señora Rodriguez an' her family, an' Otelia—remember her? She lived upstairs."

"I mean a lotta *Latinos*, Moms. Like here in the *Barrio*. And how about *morenos?*"

"*Muchacho*, they got all kind." Momma laughed. "Fat and skinny, big and little. And—"

"Okay, Momma," I said. "You win. Give me a kiss."

So we moved to Babylon, a suburb on the south shore of Long Island. Momma was right about the grass and trees. And the school, too, was nice-looking. The desks were new, not all copped up like the ones in Harlem, and the teachers were kind of friendly and not so tough-looking as those in Patrick Henry [High School].

I made some kind of friends with some paddy boys. I even tried out for the school baseball team. There were a lot of paddy boys and girls watching the tryouts and I felt like I was the only one trying out. I dropped a fly ball in the outfield to cries of "Get a basket," but at bat I shut everybody out of my mind and took a swing at the ball with all I had behind it and hit a home run. I heard the cheers and made believe I hadn't.

I played my role to the most, and the weeks turned into months. I still missed Harlem, but I didn't see it for six months. *Maybe*, I thought, *this squeeze livin' ain't as bad as Crutch said.* I decided to try the lunchtime swing session in the school gym. The Italian paddy, Angelo, had said they had hot music there. I dug the two-cents admission fee out of my pocket and made it up the walk that led to the gym.

"Two cents, please," said a little *muchacha blanca.*

"Here you are."

"Thank you," she smiled.

I returned her smile. Shit, man, Crutch was wrong.

The gym was whaling. The music was on wax, and it was a mambo. I let myself react. It felt good to give in to the natural rhythm. Maybe there were other worlds besides the mean streets, I thought. I looked around the big gym and saw some of the kids I knew a little. Some of them waved; I waved back. I noticed most of the paddy kids were dancing the mambo like stiff. Then I saw a girl I had heard called Marcia or something by the other kids. She was a pretty, well-stacked girl, with black hair and a white softness which set her hair off pretty cool. I walked over to her. "Hi," I said.

"Huh? Oh, hi."

"My first time here."

"But I've seen you before. You got Mrs. Sutton for English."

"Yeah, that's right. I meant this is my first time to the gym dance."

"I also was at the field when you smashed that ball a mile."

"That was *suerte*," I said.

"What's that?" she asked.

"What?"

"What you said—'swear-tay.' "

I laughed. "Man, that's Spanish."

"Are you Spanish? I didn't know. I mean, you don't look like what I thought a Spaniard looks like."

"I ain't a Spaniard from Spain," I explained. "I'm a Puerto Rican from Harlem."

"Oh—you talk English very well," she said.

"I told you I was born in Harlem. That's why I ain't got no Spanish accent."

"No-o, your accent is more like Jerry's."

What's she tryin' to put down? I wondered. Jerry was the colored kid who recently had moved to Bay Shore.

"Did you know Jerry?" she asked. "Probably you didn't get to meet him. I heard he moved away somewhere."

"Yeah, I know Jerry," I said softly. "He moved away because he got some girl in trouble. I know Jerry is colored and I know I got his accent. Most of us in Harlem steal from each other's language or style or stick of living. And it's *suerte*, s-u-e-r-t-e. It means 'luck.' " *Jesus, Crutch, you got my mind messed up a little. I keep thinking this broad's tryin' to tell me something shitty in a nice dirty way. I'm gonna find out.* "Your name is Marcia or something like that, eh?" I added.

"Ahuh."

"Mine's Piri. Wanna dance?"

"Well, this one is almost over."

"Next one?"

"Well, er—I, er—well, the truth is that my boyfriend is sort of jealous and—well, you know how—"

I looked at her and she was smiling. I said, "Jesus, I'm sorry. Sure, I know how it is. Man, I'd feel the same way."

She smiled and shrugged her shoulders pretty-like. I
wanted to believe her. I did believe her. I had to believe her.
"Some other time, eh?"

She smiled again, cocked her head to one side and crin-
kled her nose in answer.

"Well, take it easy," I said. "See you around."

She smiled again, and I walked away not liking what I was
feeling, and thinking that Crutch was right. I fought against
it. I told myself I was still feeling out of place here in the
middle of all these strangers, that paddies weren't as bad as
we made them out to be. I looked over my shoulder and saw
Marcia looking at me funny-like. When she saw me looking,
her face changed real fast. She smiled again. I smiled back. I
felt like I was plucking a mental daisy:

> You're right, Crutch
> You're wrong, Crutch
> You're right, Crutch
> You're wrong, Crutch.

I wanted to get outside and cop some sun and I walked
toward the door.

"Hi, Piri," Angelo called. "Where you going? It's just starting."

"Aw, it's a little stuffy," I lied. "Figured on making it over
to El Viejo's—I mean, over to the soda fountain on Main
Street."

"You mean the Greek's?"

"Yeah, that's the place."

"Wait a sec till I take a leak and I'll go over with you."

I nodded okay and followed Angelo to the john. I waited
outside for him and watched the kids dancing. My feet

tapped out time and I moved closer to the gym and I was almost inside again. Suddenly, over the steady beat of the music, I heard Marcia say, "Imagine the nerve of that black thing."

"Who?" someone asked.

"That new colored boy," said another voice.

They must have been standing just inside the gym. I couldn't see them, but I had that for-sure feeling that it was me they had in their mouths.

"Let's go, Piri," Angelo said. I barely heard him. "Hey fella," he said, "what's the matter?"

"Listen, Angelo. Jus' listen," I said stonily.

". . . do you mean just like that?" one of the kids asked.

"Ahuh," Marcia said. "Just as if I was a black girl. *Well!* He started to talk to me and what could I do except be polite and at the same time not encourage him?"

"Christ, first that Jerry bastard and now him. We're getting invaded by niggers," said a thin voice.

"You said it," said another guy. "They got some nerve. My dad says that you give them an inch them apes want to take a yard."

"He's not so bad," said a shy, timid voice. "He's a polite guy and seems to be a good athlete. And besides, I hear he's a Puerto Rican."

"Ha—he's probably passing for Puerto Rican because he can't make it for white," said the thin voice. "Ha, ha, ha."

I stood there thinking who I should hit first. *Marcia. I think I'll bust her jaw first.*

"Let's go, Piri," Angelo said. "Those creeps are so f—n' snooty that nobody is good enough for them. Especially that bitch Marcia. Her and her clique think they got gold-plated assholes."

". . . no, *really!*" a girl was saying. "I heard he's a Puerto Rican, and they're not like Neg—"

"There's no difference," said the thin voice. "He's still black."

"Come on, Piri, let's go," Angelo said. "Don't pay no mind to them."

"I guess he thought he was another Jerry," someone said.

"He really asked me to dance with him," Marcia said indignantly. "I told him that my boyfriend . . . ."

The rest of the mean sounds faded as I made it out into the sun. I walked faster and faster. I cut across the baseball field, then ran as fast as I could. I wanted to get away from the things running to mind. My lungs were hurting—not from running but from not being able to scream. After a while I sat down and looked up at the sky. How near it seemed. I heard a voice: "Piri! Holy hell, you tore up the ground running." I looked up and saw Angelo. He was huffing and out of wind. "Listen, you shouldn't let them get you down," he said, kneeling next to me. "I know how you feel."

I said to him very nicely and politely, "Do me a favor, you m—f—n' paddy, get back with your people. I don't know why the f—k you're here, unless it's to ease your—oh, man, just get the f—k outta here. I hate them. I hate you. I hate all you white motherjumps."

"I'm sorry, Piri."

"Yeah, *blanco* boy, I know. You know how I feel, ain't that right? Go on, paddy, make it."

Angelo shook his head and slowly got up. He looked at me for a second, then walked away. I dug the sky again and said to it, "I ain't ever goin' back to that f—n' school. They can shove it up their asses." I plucked the last mental daisy: *You was right, Crutch.*

barrio—the 'hood, neighborhood
blanco—white
caramba—damn it
Dios mio—my God
hijo—son
morenos—blacks, dark-skinned people
muchacha blanca—white girl
muchacho—guy
nene—child

3

OUR FAMILIES

The family is one of the central pillars of Latino culture in the United States.

OF LOVE

While historically Latino men have occupied positions of power and authority in the outside world, Latina women have held powerful positions of authority in the home. Women are responsible for passing on moral, social, and cultural values and traditions to the children. The sex roles traditionally assigned to men and women in Latino families have also been reaffirmed by the Catholic Church, which, in many instances, still insists on mother and wife as the primary roles for Latinas.

The shifting gender roles in American society have thrown these values into conflict. Many Latinas have worked outside the home, and many have begun seeking education beyond high school in colleges and universities.

The numerous *abuelitas*, or grandmothers, and mothers that populate Latino literature attest to the enduring importance of Latinas as figures of love and teachers.

JUDITH ORTIZ COFER

Born in Hormigueros, Puerto Rico, in 1952, Judith Ortiz Cofer spent her childhood and adolescence traveling between her small hometown and Paterson, New Jersey, where her father was stationed as a naval officer. In this selection, "Casa," Cofer brings to life the voice of her grandmother as she told cautionary stories about love and men to her daughters and granddaughters. These orally transmitted stories had a profound impact on the author's identity as a woman. As storytelling, they inspired her development as a writer. This selection appears in Judith Ortiz Cofer's Silent Dancing: A Partial Remembrance of a Puerto Rican Childhood (*1990*).

At three or four o'clock in the afternoon, the hour of *café con leche,* the women of my family gathered in Mamá's living room to speak of important things and to tell stories for the hundredth time, as if to each other, meant to be overheard by us young girls, their daughters. In Mamá's house (everyone called my grandmother Mamá) was a large parlor built by my grandfather to his wife's exact specifications so that it was always cool, facing away from the sun. The doorway was on the side of the house so no one could walk directly into her living room. First they had to take a little stroll through and around her beautiful garden where prize-winning orchids grew in the trunk of an ancient tree she had hollowed out for that purpose. This room was furnished with several mahogany rocking chairs, acquired at the births of her children, and one intricately carved rocker that had passed down to Mamá at the death of her own mother. It was on these rockers that my mother, her sisters and my grandmother sat on these afternoons of my childhood to tell their stories, teaching each other and my cousin and me what it was like to be a woman, more specifically, a Puerto Rican woman. They talked about life on the island, and life in *Los Nueva Yores*, their way of referring to the U.S., from New York City to California: the other place, not home, all the same. They told real-life stories, though as I later learned, always embellishing them with a little or a lot of dramatic detail, and they told *cuentos*, the morality and cautionary tales told by the women in our family for generations: stories that became a part of my subconscious as I grew up in two worlds, the tropical island and the cold city, and which would later surface in my dreams and in my poetry.

One of these tales was about the woman who was left at the altar. Mamá liked to tell that one with histrionic intensity. I remember the rise and fall of her voice, the sighs, and her constantly gesturing hands, like two birds swooping through her words. This particular story would usually come up in a conversation as a result of someone mentioning a forthcoming engagement or wedding. The first time I remember hearing it, I was sitting on the floor at Mamá's feet, pretending to read a comic book. I may have been eleven or twelve years old: at that difficult age when a girl is no longer a child who can be ordered to leave the room if the women wanted freedom to take their talk into forbidden zones, or really old enough to be considered a part of their conclave. I could only sit quietly, pretending to be in another world, while absorbing it all in a sort of unspoken agreement of my status as silent auditor. On this day, Mamá had taken my long, tangled mane of hair into her ever busy hands. Without looking down at me or interrupting her flow of words, she began braiding my hair, working at it with the quickness and determination which characterized all her actions. My mother was watching us impassively from her rocker across the room. On her lips played a little ironic smile. I would never sit still for *her* ministrations, but even then, I instinctively knew that she did not possess Mamá's matriarchal power to command and keep everyone's attention. This was particularly evident in the spell she cast when telling a story.

"It is not like it used to be when I was a girl," Mamá announced. "Then, a man could leave a girl standing at the church altar with a bouquet of fresh flowers in her hands and disappear off the face of the earth. No way to track him down if he was from another town. He could be a married man, with maybe even two or three families all over the island. There was no way to know. And there were men who did this. *Hombres* with the devil in their flesh who would come to a pueblo, like this one, take a job at one of the *haciendas*, never meaning to stay, only to have a good time and to seduce the women."

The whole time she was speaking, Mamá was weaving my hair into a flat plait which required pulling apart the two sections of hair with little jerks that made my eyes water; but knowing how Grandmother detested whining and *boba* (sissy) tears, as she called them, I just sat up as straight and stiff as I did at La Escuela San José, where the nuns enforced good posture with a flexible plastic ruler they bounced off slumped shoulders and heads. As Mamá's story progressed, I noticed how my young aunt Laura had lowered her eyes, refusing to meet Mamá's meaningful gaze. Laura was seventeen, in her last year of high school, and already engaged to a boy from another town who had staked his claim with a tiny diamond ring, then left for Los Nueva Yores to make his fortune. They were planning to get married in a year; but Mamá had expressed serious doubts that the wedding would ever take place. In Mamá's eyes, a man set free without a legal contract was a man lost. She believed that marriage was not something men desired, but simply the price they had to pay for the privilege of children, and of course, for what no decent (synonymous with "smart") woman would give away for free. "María la Loca was only seventeen when *it* happened to her." I listened closely at the mention of this name. María was a town "character," a fat middle-aged woman who lived with her old mother on the outskirts of town. She was to be seen around the pueblo delivering the meat pies the two women made for a living. The most peculiar thing about María, in my eyes, was that she walked and moved like a little girl, though she had the thick body and wrinkled face of an old woman. She would swing her hips in an exaggerated, clownish way, and some-times even hop and skip up to someone's house. She spoke to no one. Even if you asked her a question, she would just look at you and smile, showing her yellow teeth. But I had heard that if you got close enough, you could hear her humming a tune without words. The kids yelled out nasty things at her, calling her *la Loca*, and the men who hung out at the bodega playing dominoes sometimes whistled mock-ingly as she passed by with her funny, outlandish walk. But María seemed impervious to it all, carrying her basket of *pasteles* like a grotesque Little Red Riding Hood through the forest.

María la Loca interested me, as did all the eccentrics and "crazies" of our pueblo. Their weirdness was a measuring stick I used in my serious quest for a definition of "normal."

As a Navy brat, shuttling between New Jersey and the pueblo, I was constantly made to feel like an oddball by my peers, who made fun of my two-way accent: a Spanish accent when I spoke English; and, when I spoke Spanish, I was told that I sounded like a "*Gringa.*" Being the outsiders had already turned my brother and me into cultural chameleons, developing early the ability to blend into a crowd, to sit and read quietly in a fifth-story apartment building for days and days when it was too bitterly cold to play outside; or, set free, to run wild in Mamá's realm, where she took charge of our lives, releasing Mother for a while from the intense fear for our safety that our father's absences instilled in her. In order to keep us from harm when Father was away, Mother kept us under strict surveillance. She even walked us to and from Public School No. 11, which we attended during the months we lived in Paterson, New Jersey, our home base in the States. Mamá freed the three of us like pigeons from a cage. I saw her as my liberator and my model. Her stories were parables from which to glean the *Truth.*

"María la Loca was once a beautiful girl. Everyone thought she would marry the Méndez boy." As everyone knew, Rogelio Méndez was no other than the richest man in town. "But," Mamá continued, knitting my hair with the same intensity she was putting into her story, "this *macho* made a fool out of her and ruined her life." She paused for the effect of her use of the word "macho," which at that time had not yet become a popular epithet for an unliberated man. This word had for us the crude and comical connotation of "male of the species," stud; a *macho* was what you put in a pen to increase your stock.

I peeked over my comic book at my mother. She too was under Mamá's spell, smiling conspiratorially at this little swipe at men. She was safe from Mamá's contempt in this area. Married at an early age, an unspotted lamb, she had been accepted by a good family of strict Spaniards whose name was old and respected, though their fortune had been lost long before my birth. In a rocker Papá had painted sky blue sat Mamá's oldest child, Aunt Nena. Mother of three children, stepmother of two more, she was a quiet woman who liked books but had married an ignorant and abusive widower whose main interest in life was accumulating wealth. He too was in the mainland working on his dream of returning home rich and triumphant to buy the *finca* of his dreams. She was waiting for him to send for her. She would leave her children with Mamá for several years while the two of them slaved away in factories. He would one day be a rich man, and she a sadder woman. Even now her life-light was dimming. She spoke little, an aberration in Mamá's house, and she read avidly, as if storing up spiritual food for the long winters that awaited her in Los Nueva Yores without her family. But even Aunt Nena came alive to Mama's words, rocking gently, her hands over a thick book in her lap. Her daughter, my cousin Sara, played jacks by herself on the tile porch outside the room where we sat. She was a year older than I. We shared a bed and all our family's secrets. Collaborators in search of answers, Sara and I discussed everything we heard the women say, trying to fit it all together like a puzzle that once assembled would reveal life's mysteries to us. Though she and I still enjoyed taking part in boys' games—chase, volleyball and even *vaqueros,* the island version of cowboys and Indians involving camp-gun battles and violent shootouts under the mango tree in Mamá's backyard—we loved best the quiet hours in the afternoon when the men were still at work and the boys had gone to play serious baseball at the park. Then Mamá's house belonged only to us women. The aroma of coffee perking in the kitchen, the mesmerizing creaks and groans of the rockers, and the women telling their lives in *cuentos* are forever woven into the fabric of my imagination, braided like my hair that day I felt my grandmother's hands teaching me about strength, her voice convincing me of the power of storytelling.

That day Mamá told of how the beautiful María had fallen prey to a man whose name was never the same in subsequent versions of the story; it was Juan one time, José, Rafael, Diego, another. We understood that the name, and really any of the facts, were not important, only that a woman had allowed love to defeat her. Mamá put each of us in María's place by describing her wedding dress in loving detail: how she looked like a princess in her lace as she waited at the altar. Then, as Mamá approached the tragic denouement of her story, I was distracted by the sound of my aunt Laura's violent rocking. She seemed on the verge of tears. She knew the fable was intended for her. That week she was going to have her wedding gown fitted, though no firm date had been set for the marriage. Mamá ignored Laura's obvious discomfort, digging out a ribbon from the sewing basket she kept by her rocker while describing María's long illness, "a fever that would not break for days." She spoke of a mother's despair: "That woman climbed the church steps on her knees every morning, wore only black as a *promesa* to the Holy Virgin in exchange for her daughter's health." By the time María returned from her honey-moon with death, she was ravished, no longer young or sane. "As you can see she is almost as old as her mother already," Mamá lamented while tying the ribbon to the ends of my hair, pulling it back with such force that I just knew that I would never be able to close my eyes completely again.

"That María is getting crazier every day." Mamá's voice would take a lighter tone now, expressing satisfaction, either for the perfection of my braid, or for a story well told; it was hard to tell. "You know that tune she is always humming?" Carried away by her enthusiasm, I tried to nod, but Mamá would still have me pinned between her knees.

"Well, that's the wedding march." Surprising us all, Mamá sang out, "*Da, da, dará . . . da, da, dará.*" Then lifting me off the floor by my skinny shoulders, she led me around the room in an impromptu waltz—another session ending with the laughter of women, all of us caught up in the infectious joke of our lives.

café con leche—coffee with milk, cappuccino-style

finca—farm

Gringa—perjorative term for an Anglo woman

haciendas—ranches

hombres—men

la Loca—the Crazy Woman

pasteles—a Puerto Rican dish that somewhat resembles Mexican tamales. They are made with plantain flour and a meat filling, then wrapped in banana-tree leaves and boiled

promesa—promise

OF DEATH

The traditional roles assigned to men and women in Latino families have also clashed with the reality of homosexuality and AIDS. Of epidemic proportions among Latinos—and particularly among Latinas—AIDS has brought into our consciousness a new sense of family that differs from the traditional nuclear model of father, mother, and children.

Most Latinos and Latinas know someone who is infected with HIV or who has died of AIDS, leading many to re-examine their own attitudes toward gays, drug addicts and prostitutes, and toward the numerous others who have contracted the disease. This epidemic has also created new avenues for political struggle, as many HIV-positive Latinos have to face double prejudices from society and the medical profession. Unfortunately, discussion of AIDS and homosexuality remains taboo among many adults in Latino communities.

RUBÉN MARTÍNEZ

This selection, "A Death in the Family," is a compelling portion from a chapter about AIDS from The Other Side, *a collection of short chronicles and poems about life in Los Angeles written by Salvadoran journalist and poet Rubén Martínez.*

The story of Sergio's death from AIDS illustrates the tensions between his parents, the traditional family in Mexico, and the family that has resulted from his union with his gay lover Daniel in Los Angeles. This piece also shows the denial, the pain, and the renewed spiritual strength that we all develop in the face of death.

❦ *Los Angeles, March 1988*

*Sergio is wearing jeans with two jagged holes at the knees, a
T-shirt with suspenders, and a red bandana headband: he's
both punk and* vato. *His face is expressive and mercurial: a
hard look gives way to a quirky smile, blends into a distant
gaze.*

Daniel Lara presses the fast-forward button on the VCR.
He eases himself back in his chair and props his head upon
his hand, silently watching the accelerated images of Sergio's birthday party ripple across the screen. He says that he
is looking for a specific image that will show me Sergio "at
his best." He lets the tape roll at normal speed for a few
moments.

*Sergio's family and friends are gathered in the backyard
of a modest* barrio *home on a sunny afternoon. The children
shout and dash about. Someone puts on some music—a*
cumbia *rhythm. Sergio beams. He gets up to dance.*

"This is what I wanted you to see," says Daniel.

*Only a few people follow Sergio's lead. The rest are still
seated, content to watch. As he bends his knees, his skin
shows through the holes in his Levis. He smiles, tosses his
head back like an outrageously proud macho, and then he
swings his hips exaggeratedly, sensually.*

"Isn't that incredible?" says Daniel. "Here he is, being,
what's the word? So *fruity.* And yet his family—they're completely okay with it!"

*Close-ups of the faces of the family members seated
around the impromptu dance floor. There is some laughter,
perhaps from mild embarrassment, but not a single face
betrays ill feelings. Sergio closes his eyes, stretches his arms
wide, opens his palms and twirls about. . . .*

The offices of AIDS Project Los Angeles (APLA) don't exactly make you feel you're in a protective environment; they have a corporate feel to them, and you could mistake the ambience for that of an insurance firm. In Daniel Lara's office (he is program manager for community education here) the strains of a Mexican *balada* emerge from a small tape deck. . . .

Daniel had met Sergio five years ago, and soon afterward they began living together, he tells me, his face slightly pale above the growth of a new beard. They had come from completely different worlds. Sergio grew up in Mexico City's *barrios,* a boy who became aware of being different at an early age. And it was as if Sergio's very body was at the center of the relentless conflict of growing up gay in such an eminently anti-gay environment as Mexico—from his early years, he suffered from numerous physical maladies. At age ten, there was rheumatic fever. Before he was out of his teens, he'd suffered a heart attack. Later there was open heart surgery, two strokes.

"He knew that if he were ever going to be truly happy with himself, he would have to be somewhere where he could be free of the prejudices and negative stereotypes about gay men in Mexico," says Daniel.

In coming to Los Angeles and meeting Daniel, Sergio had been able to establish his independence firmly. But that success had not been achieved overnight. Once here, Sergio followed a path familiar to many, if not most, Latin American immigrants. Although he finished a *preparatoria* education in Mexico (equivalent to junior college in the United States) and attained a degree in accounting, the language barrier and the fact that his credentials weren't transferable meant that Sergio found himself on the bottom rung of the socioeconomic ladder. He worked as a short-order cook at a Burrito King to make ends meet. But his ambitious nature led him to take night courses at Roosevelt Bilingual School, where he polished his English. Classes at East Los Angeles College came next. His goal was a management-level job.

When finally he landed a job as a telephone operator at the Department of Motor Vehicles (DMV), it wasn't exactly management, but it was a start. Sergio fell ill around that time, however. Although he soon recovered from what he would later discover had been the beginning of an ARC (AIDS-Related Complex) condition, he lost his job at the DMV. The official diagnosis of full-blown AIDS came in August 1986.

"He looked at AIDS—and I've never been able to reconcile myself with this—as a gift," says Daniel. "He said that AIDS for him was an affirmation, a sign that God had not abandoned him." Sergio's traditional Catholicism—highly ironic, considering the Church's official anti-gay attitude—was a catalyst for Daniel. He had grown up in the States and flirted with Chicano Movement politics in its heyday, but had ultimately opted for a secular and professional existence well within the American mainstream. Meeting Sergio, Daniel says, was like "hitting a brick wall."

"He was very tied to religion. He had his *velas* [votive candles], and he had his *santos* [Saints], and he had his *medallas* [religious medallions], his *hierbas*, his holy water and his *oraciones*; all of these were things that I'd lost." Daniel smiles as he recites the list in Spanish. "I now have the *velas*, I have Sergio's *santos*, I have his *hierbas*."

When Sergio's mother came up from Mexico City to visit her son soon after his AIDS diagnosis, she faced his homosexuality openly for the first time. She told him that she would not speak to him until after he "changed his lifestyle," Daniel remembers. More than a year would pass without contact between mother and son. Sergio's father never knew about his son's gay lifestyle; nor would he ever learn that he had AIDS.

As his health worsened, Sergio came more and more into contact with a health establishment little prepared to handle the AIDS crisis. At the time of his diagnosis, APLA was practically the only resource available to persons with AIDS, regardless of ethnic or class background. And in Sergio's view, APLA was doing little, if anything at all, for Latinos with AIDS. He began to complain—to anyone who'd listen—about what he saw as a discriminatory situation.

Sergio's illness and activist sentiment spurred Daniel to take action by offering his services to APLA. Although the agency is considered by many activists to be part of the AIDS "establishment," Daniel felt that the best way to influence it was by working within the system, accepting its sometimes sluggish nature. But Sergio, always the rebel, took the opposite approach.

"Whereas we would say, 'You have to deal with the system,' he would say, 'No you don't; you can fight.' " Sergio often went straight to APLA's top administration—over Daniel's head—demanding, among other things, that APLA bilingualize its services. Sergio also lobbied for bereavement counseling in Spanish to help an AIDS victim's family deal with the impact of the disease, something he considered essential for family-oriented Latino culture and its particular brand of homophobia.

Sergio literally took his message to the streets. He gave dozens of public *platicas*, informal talks, on AIDS at churches, schools, hospitals, "anywhere they'd take us," says Daniel. He would talk about his life experiences, about the poor treatment he'd received in hospitals, about the need for more education and AIDS services for Latinos. But most important, says Daniel, Sergio's message was "that his goal was to live, and, cliché as it sounds, that AIDS was the disease, and that faith was the cure."

In the fall, Daniel began noticing that Sergio was suffering lapses of memory and other signs of dementia. Still, Sergio mustered enough strength to join the hundreds of thousands of gay men and women who marched on Washington, D.C., in October, calling for a government response to the AIDS crisis.

It was in November, Daniel says, that he lost the Sergio he'd known and loved. By December, Sergio was bedridden, almost continually delirious. Daniel phoned Sergio's mother in Mexico City, and she was soon at her son's bedside, no longer complaining about his "lifestyle" but taking care of his every need as she did when he was a baby.

Sergio's mother and Daniel decided to place him on a morphine drip, without any other treatment, as a way of letting him die without any more unnecessary suffering. On December 12, a traditional Mexican holiday in honor of the Virgen de Guadalupe, Sergio was lucid for a few hours. Daniel took the opportunity to tell him of their decision. "He put both of his hands on my face," Daniel says, now placing his hands on his cheeks. "He said to me, 'How can you help me to live, if you are so negative? You have to believe me when I tell you that I will get over this, that this will pass, and I can't do it unless you're on my side.' "

Latinos at a candlelight AIDS vigil in New York City. The AIDS epidemic has had a profound impact on all Latino communities throughout the United States.

One day in early January, Sergio told Daniel: "You don't believe me when I tell you that I won't die." In retrospect, Daniel says, "I think he meant it in the spiritual sense. That his spirit would continue to be here. I only focused on the physical."

Sergio died the next day.

At the service, there was anything but morbidity. Daniel had wanted a celebration, and there indeed was one, with mariachi music and a large gathering of friends. Daniel had thought that only such a ceremony would befit what Sergio would surely have believed was his passing into the After-life.

Daniel boarded the plane in Los Angeles dressed in black. Sergio's family greeted him at the airport in Mexico City dressed in black. He had known that the "celebration of life" in L.A. was the opposite of what he would encounter in Mexico. The open grief that he found among Sergio's family was anathema to Daniel. He feared that if he gave in to the sorrow, he wouldn't be able to control himself . . . and then what? Have the family about him wonder why he cried like a wife over a dead husband?

Daniel accompanied Sergio's family and friends to the mausoleum to place the ashes in the crypt. En route, he carried the box containing the ashes in his lap. He held it all the way to the mausoleum, causing an invisible but extremely uncomfortable tension between him and Sergio's mother.

"May I have my son?" she asked Daniel in front of the crypt.

Daniel hesitated. He ran his hand along the box, and slowly handed it to her. She placed the ashes in the crypt, knelt and said her goodbyes. Sergio's father did the same, then his sister. Two workers were about to set in place the stone that would seal the crypt forever when Daniel asked them to wait. He knelt down, and with his hand reached into the space for a moment, as if to retrieve Sergio. But his hand came out empty, and with it he drew the sign of the cross before the crypt.

balada—ballad
cumbia—a style of celebratory music based on the African
     cumbe dance and song
hierbas—herbs
oraciones—prayers
vato—cool dude

OF LOVE BEFORE DEATH

While traditional values can play a negative role in accepting difference, the human strength that comes from tradition, loyalty, and a deep sense of commitment among Latinos is most evident in our elders. Unlike Anglo families, many Latinos live in extended families that include their grandparents and even great-grandparents. Elders are much respected and admired by the young and by adults, for they symbolize strength in the face of the struggles for survival that Latinos have experienced collectively. Taking care of their elders, Latinos practice a moral sense of responsibility toward others that highly characterizes their family values.

PAT MORA

Pat Mora, a well-known Chicana poet, was born in El Paso, Texas. She is the author of a number of poetry collections, including Borders *and* Chants, *for which she received the Southwest Book Award. Her poetry has been hailed as "a healing voice," and the poem that follows, "Los Ancianos," sings to the strength and beauty of an older Mexican couple who have been married for fifty years. The poem describes them in Mexico, where their love transcends time and place, in contrast to the modern values of materialism and mobility symbolized in the figures of the passing tourists.*

 They hold hands
as they walk with slow steps.
Careful together they cross the plaza
both slightly stooped, bodies returning to the land,
he in faded khaki and straw hat,
she wrapped in soft clothes, black
rebozo round her head and shoulders.

Tourists in halter tops and shorts
pose by flame trees and fountains,
but the old couple walks step by step
on the edge.
Even in the heat, only their wrinkled
hands and faces show. They know
of moving through a crowd at their own pace.

I watch him help her
off the curb and I smell love
like dried flowers, old love
of holding hands with one man for fifty years.

Los Ancianos—the elderly couple, the elderly
rebozo—shawl

4

OUR FAITHS

The Spanish conquest imposed the religion of Roman Catholicism on the Indian populations of Central and Latin America. Today, while the majority of Latinos remain Catholic, many have found spiritual fulfillment as members of other churches—Adventist, Baptist, Pentecostal, Mormon— that have been evangelizing rural areas of Latin America since the turn of the twentieth century. An important religious movement has also been Liberation Theology, an overtly political branch of Catholicism that seeks to empower the poor with the knowledge and tools needed for liberation from economic hardship and political tyranny. All of these religious trends and practices are alive among Latino communities in the United States.

FOLKWAYS

Catholicism has remained the dominant religion in Latino cultures throughout our hemisphere because it has been practiced along with the values and beliefs of Indian religions and the faiths that Africans brought with them as slaves. *Santería* in the Caribbean and Brazil, where it is known as *Candomble*, combines the worship of Catholic saints with African deities. In Mexico, Catholics attend mass every Sunday but also go to *curanderos*, or healers, who practice folk religion.

ALAN WEST

Like many other Latino writers and artists, Alan West has drawn on the myths and symbols associated with Santería's gods to fuel his art. This poem, "The Forest of Desire," tells the story of four deities, Oggún, Oshún, Yemayá, and Changó. Part of the pantheon of the Yoruba tribe of West Africa, they continued to be worshiped by Africans when they were brought to the Americas as slaves. Here the deities became major figures in Santería. Oggún is the god of metal, wars, and hospitals. Oshún is the goddess of rivers, and Yemayá, Oshún's sister, is the goddess of the sea and fertility. And Changó is the god of thunder and music. Alan West was born in Havana, Cuba, in 1953 and raised in Puerto Rico. He is a poet, journalist, critic, translator, and author of children's books on Roberto Clemente and José Martí.

Oggún had seen
too much strife.
He saw only
steel in men's eyes,
the flash of blades
and splitting flesh.
Oggún yearned for water

but always saw blood.
Oggún didn't know anymore
who were the dead
and who were the living.
So he fled the living and
the dead and went into
the forest to live with
snakes, lions and monkeys.

Danger was near
and Oggún was needed
for the blacksmiths and warriors.
But no one had seen him for years.
A *guemilere* was started to see
if he would come out of the forest.
The *batá* drums pounded
day and night, day and night,
but the forest remained silent.

Yemayá said, "Play the drums
for my sister, there is a river
that runs through the forest."

And the batás began again,
swallowing trees and earth,
roots and flowers,
swelling into the river
until Oshún appeared,
dancing and singing with
her five yellow handkerchiefs.
She sang to the lions, the birds,
the snakes, the moles
and to Oggún, who was

invisible as an ant.
Oshún stopped dancing and singing.
She ordered the drums to stop.

Silently, she went into the forest.
Oggún was sitting quietly
dressed in green and black
talking to the snakes.
Oshún drew closer and began
to dance.
Oggún was scared,
but he drew closer.
Oshún began to sing.
Oggún drew closer but she
paid no attention,
her feet were like butterflies,
her ankles made sounds like bells,
her thighs shimmered with light,
and from her waist swayed a
honey-filled gourd.
Oggún drew closer and Oshún
dipped her fingers in the gourd
and spread sweet *oñí* onto Oggún's lips.

Oggún couldn't move.
Only his waist moved, surrounded
by yellow handkerchiefs.
She danced like a bird and sang
and spread *oñí* all over Oggún's face.

She had five mirrors on her
which moved like warriors' masks,
a fountain of steel and light.

She dropped bits of pumpkin on the path
and dancing and singing, drew him to the village,
leaving a trail of handkerchiefs and honey.

The villagers and the *orishas* welcomed Oggún back.
Oggún was stunned, still weak from dancing and
the honey.
He asked for Oshún, his undying love.
He went to the river to bring her back.
But Oshún had eyes only for Changó.

The warriors and the blacksmiths carried Oggún
on their shoulders.
Oggún wanted to look for the mirrors,
but when he saw them
they only showed him the river, singing and dancing.

batá—a double-sided drum played on the lap and used for
  sacred purposes
guemilere—a drum-playing session used to invoke spirits
oñí—honey
Orisha—a Yoruba deity

JUANITA SEDILLO
*In contrast to their lack of participation in the Catholic
Church, women have been central in practicing and trans-
mitting values and beliefs in folk religions. Juanita Sedillo, a*
curandera, *or folk healer, from New Mexico, recounts at age
eighty-three how healing skills were passed on from woman
to woman in her family. The practices that she describes
have been an alternative for many Latinos who cannot
afford health care and don't trust modern medicine.*

🙰🙰 My grandmother, my mother's mother, was a *curandera*. We never saw a doctor, but they would treat us, and we would get better. If we got a fever or flu, or whatever we caught, they took care of us with herbs and we got better.

From them we all learned a little about medicine. From our great-grandmothers and then our grandmothers. There's always new *curanderas* who teach the next generation, and that's how the art continues, see? That's how I became a *curandera*. I also learned to heal and deliver babies from a woman in Montecello who was a *curandera* and a midwife.

I began in 1930, 1931. A woman on the ranch where we lived was very ill, and a neighbor came to me for help. I said to him, "Well, I don't know." I didn't know anything [about healing], but I went. She was very sick with pneumonia. [I thought to myself,] "Yes, but what can I do for her? I don't know, but I'll try hard." Perhaps it was God who told me, "Mix menthol with cinnamon." I mixed them, and rubbed it on her, and then put a hot towel on her. She got better. Strange. Maybe God put it into my mind to make that remedy for that woman.

Later I learned to deliver babies, and I kept on. What I treat most often is *empacho* (stomachache). Most people who come to see me have digestive problems, or a pain in their side, or a headache. For *empacho*, I massage their stomachs and pull their skin. Then I give them the medicine, and from that, they get rid of the *empacho*. The same for an inflammation. I massage the area a little bit, and then I give them medicine to dissolve the inflammation. I make my medicines solely from herbs, Mexican herbs. That is all you need—that is the reason God put all those herbs on the earth.

When I delivered babies, I gave the women a bit of pepper dissolved in water to help them push. Or raisins. You boil them and then use the broth. It helps them push. Afterwards, I gave them tea made from *hipazote* or *chimajá* to clean them out. I've also helped a lot of barren women have children. You have to warm their womb. Their wombs are cold, and as long as they're cold they can't conceive. I've helped a lot of women, but sometimes it's the husband who can't have children.

I've healed all kinds of people—women, men, children. Illness from fright is what I cure most. My son, Siriaco, had very weak blood. When he was in the army they put some kind of spell on him, and he wrote me to send him medicine. I sent him *oshá* and a few grains of roasted salt. All you need is *oshá* and salt. You spit on them, and then you wrap them up.

A lot of people don't believe in such a thing as the evil eye, but you can cast a spell, sometimes even without knowing it. Once when my son was in the army, my cousin Iginio began to tease me. He was always saying how lucky I was that Siriaco was in the army. Just teasing. I didn't even know that I was angry, because he used to tease me like that all the time. But I guess he got me mad that day—and the result was that he lost his speech. My aunt laughed and told me to get some pieces of nuts and put them on his tongue. I told him to stick out his tongue, and I covered it with the ground nuts. Then he could talk again. After that, my cousin would always say, "Don't bother her, because she'll leave you mute."

I have cured all types of illnesses. I've traveled all over, all the way to Albuquerque. People would come all the way

from Albuquerque to get me to heal someone. And I have
taught others. I tell them, "Look, this remedy is for this, and
this one is for that, and so on." Now that I've taught others
how to do it, I don't work much anymore. When someone
comes to see me, I send them to my daughter-in-law to be
healed.

People ask me why I don't heal myself. Well, I try. I make
all the medicines that I know are good. But maybe God
doesn't want me to get better anymore. Nothing guarantees
that I'll be here tomorrow.

chimajá—Indian parsley, used to heal stomach ailments
curandera—folk healer
hipazote—an herb from the American wormseed plant
oshá—Porter's lovage, an herb common in New Mexico,
   used for healing colds and other conditions

THE CHURCH

For young Latinos and Latinas growing up in the Catholic
faith, the Church exerts a powerful influence in daily life,
particularly if they attend Catholic schools. This influence
shows itself in, among other things, preparation for and
practice of the ritual of First Communion.

Although an important ritual for any young Catholic, First
Communion for a Latino seems to acquire added significance. For the young boy or girl, First Communion is often
the occasion of receiving his or her first specially tailored
suit or dress. First Communion celebrations can be large
parties including friends and extended family members. Because of the extra emphasis, First Communion can also be
an extremely stressful experience.

Latinas making their First Communion. An important ritual for any Catholic, the First Communion carries particular significance in many Latino communities and serves as a sign of the powerful role the Catholic Church plays in Latinos' lives.

EDWARD RIVERA

In this excerpt from Family Installments, *a novel about growing up Puerto Rican in New York City, Edward Rivera writes of such a stressful First Communion experience. With a humor that borders on irreverence, the speaker, Santos Malánguez, gives a blow-by-blow account of an especially botched ritual.*

While I was waiting there, turning to stone, or salt, or liquid, someone grabbed my arm, the same spot where Sister had pinched it. It was still sore. "Don't move." It was her voice again, down low. It sounded like something out of a cowboy movie I'd seen with Papi. "Okay, Malánguezzz, don't move. This is a chodown."

She was only getting me ready for the walk to the railing. She held me there in a tight grip for about ten seconds, and as soon as one of the kneeling receivers, looking no better than before, had made a stiff about-face and started solemnly back to his pew with the Host in his mouth, Sister pointed a finger at the opening and told me to go get It, before one of Sister Haughney's girls beat me to It. Then she let go my arm, and it was as if she had pressed a button or released a spring I didn't know I had: I took off for that railing like a hungry dog tearing ass for a bowl of chow. But there was a lot of "chow" for everyone. Father Rooney's ciborium was stacked, and there was plenty more Host back in the tabernacle. One of the assisting priests, Father Mooney, had already replaced Father Rooney's empty ciborium with a fresh ciborium, and was standing by in front of the altar, waiting for another nod from the railing.

"Walk, Ssantoss Malánguezzz, don't run!" Sister hizzed behind me. Too late. I was already kneeling at the railing, hands joined under my chin. She'd get me tomorrow morning. Maybe in the auditorium. Special assembly for the execution. Organ music and chorus.

And then Father Rooney and his other assistant were on top of me with the ciborium. The assistant stuck a golden plate with a handle under my chin—a paten, it was called, a metallic bib just in case. Father Rooney was holding the Host between thumb and index and wagging It in front of my mouth, which suddenly wouldn't open. Lockjaw from fright. My punishment for cursing in church.

"Open your mouth, young man," Father Rooney suggested. We hadn't rehearsed this part.

I used both hands to do it: one hand under my nose, the other pushing down on my chin. But then my tongue wouldn't come out for the presence. The spit in my mouth had thickened and turned to glue, and my tongue was stuck to my palate.

"Stick out your tongue," the priest with the paten said.

I stuck two fingers in my mouth and unstuck my tongue.

"What's he doing, Matt?" Father Rooney asked his assistant.

"You got me, Mark. What are you doing, kid?"

"I am sorry, Father," I said. "The tongue got stuck to the—"

"Shh! You're not supposed to talk in here during Mass," the pastor said. He wasn't looking too happy.

"I am sorry, Father," I said automatically, trying to get the spit going again.

"Out with the tongue, son," Father Matt repeated. "Or leave the railing."

I closed my eyes and did as he said. Then Father Rooney delivered his Latin lines: "*Corpus Domini nostri Jesu Christi custodiat animam tuam,* etcetera. Amen." ["May the body

of our Lord Jesus Christ guard your soul."] Father Matt had
his paten under my chin—cold metal—and I felt a familiar
warm dribble working its way down my thigh, spoiling my
fresh pair of First Communion shorts. The whole place was
looking on, except possibly Papi and Mami, who must have
been staring down at their hands in embarrassment. Then
the worst of all possible things happened: the Host broke in
half on my nose. I still had my eyes shut, so I didn't see just
how Father Rooney managed to do it but I could figure it
out. I must have made him nervous, and instead of slapping
It down on the tip of my tongue, he caught the tip of my
nose, and the presence broke in two. One half stayed in
Father Rooney's fingers, and the other floated past my
tongue, bounced off the railing, missing Father Matt's paten
altogether, and came to a stop on the symbol-crowded rug
on their side of the railing, between Father Matt's shoes,
which were barely visible under his alb, as Sister Felicia had
called that fancy undergarment.

Both priests gasped at the same time and crossed themselves. Everyone in church, except for the sleeping winos in
the back, must have done the same thing. Padilla's organ
began playing *"En Mi Viejo San Juan,"* a golden oldie,
probably to distract everyone from the horrible accident I'd
just caused at the railing. And my bladder was having itself a
time with my new shorts. Father Matt stooped quickly, with
his paten held tight to his heart, and started looking for the
half-Host. I remembered what Sister had said about "His
body broken in pieces" is why something-something, and
felt horrible. The people who had nailed Him to the Cross
couldn't have felt worse afterwards than I did just then.

Father Matt was still down on his knees looking for It. He
was getting warm. I could have told him, but I was afraid to
open my mouth. He was saying something under his breath,

and Father Rooney, all out of patience, said, "Just pick It up, Matt. We'll be here all day at this rate."

"Sorry, Mark," said Father Matt. "Here It is." He used his paten as a dust pan to scoop It up, nudging It with his index finger. It broke again during this delicate recovery, but that didn't matter. You could split It up into a couple of hundred pieces, and It was still one. That was part of the mystery behind It. The "accidents" were one thing, Sister had told us; the "essence" was something else. You couldn't violate *that*. She had told us about an egg named Humpty Dumpty to illustrate the difference between a "material" object, in this case a talking egg, and the mysterious "indivisible Host."

Just the same I was having my doubts. One piece was in Father Rooney's chalice (he had slipped it back inside when no one was looking), and the other half was down there, getting scooped up by Father Matt; and I was having trouble understanding how both pieces were one and the same. Sister Felicia would tell me all about it first thing tomorrow morning, in front of everyone. I wanted to go back home. I wanted no part of this business; I was unfit, unworthy, un-everything, but I was frozen there on my knees, terrified.

Father Matt finally got back to his feet, the paten with the two extra pieces held against his chest, and the thumb and index finger of his other hand pinning Them down to prevent another accident. Then Father Rooney held out his ciborium, which looked like a fancy trophy to me—it had jewels in the middle and was made of gold, or something that resembled gold—and Father Matt nudged the two pieces into it. I thought Father Rooney was going to slap a fresh sample on my tongue, but he had nothing like that in mind. I didn't even get the three broken pieces. I had my tongue out again, but all I got was a piece of advice. "Go back to your pew, kid," he told me. "You're not ready to receive."

And Father Matt said, "Grow up, son. You're seven already." I was eight, already one year behind, and no end in sight. And then he turned to Father Rooney and said, in a whisper, "This whole neighborhood's going to the—"

But Father Rooney cut him short: "Not here, Matt. Later, in the rectory."

"You're the boss, Mark." And off they went to plant an intact presence on Grippe's tongue. The worst disgrace in my life to date; and once you started in with the disgraces, it was hard to stop. Some types couldn't do a thing right. They talked in church when they should have been praying in silence, they cursed before receiving, they didn't know their own neck size, or the size of their feet, and they conned their parents into paying for half their First Communion outfits, just to insult Sister. And now this. In public, too. Hundreds had seen it. Maybe a thousand. And my own parents sitting in the back, next to Saint Anthony and his lilies, pretending they didn't know who I was. At least I thought they were pretending. I wanted them to.

Sister Felicia helped me up to my feet and turned me around toward the pews. She walked back there with me, slowly, because my knees seemed to have run out of the oil that makes knees work and my shoes felt like something poured from cement. Heavy construction. She led me back to my pew by the arm she'd pinched, and as she was sitting me down she put her mouth to my ear and said, "Ssantoss Malánguezzz, you are a disgrace to our school," bearing down on "disgrace." "You are not fit for First Communion, and maybe never will be. We have a lot to discuss tomorrow morning."

I nodded; but did she think I was going to show up at school next morning? Even as I sat there in my wet shorts, my mind was out in Central Park playing hooky next day. They were going to get me anyway, day after next, no way out of it; but in the meantime I thought I was entitled to a day of rest and I was going to take it. Maybe they'd send me to P.S. Genghis Khan, where I'd have no trouble blending in with the "barbarians," which might not be a bad idea.

"En Mi Viejo San Juan"—"In My Old San Juan," composed by Noel Estrada, a popular nostalgic song about leaving Puerto Rico

FOLKWAYS AND THE CHURCH

Common among Latino Catholics is the belief that saints, if prayed to, become involved in people's lives. Although non-Latino Catholics also hold this belief, it, like the First Communion, has a special significance for Latinos.

This belief reflects the influence of Indian and African religions on Catholicism among Latinos. In many instances, these religions maintained that supernatural forces could indeed be called upon to change the course of everyday events. When the Indian and African slave populations of Central and Latin America were converted to Catholicism, they were able to continue this belief by petitioning saints instead of their ancestors' gods and goddesses. In Latino communities, this practice is known as making *votos*, or promises, to saints in exchange for favors. Making *votos* has remained an important strategy for survival, even in modern times, by helping Latinos, particularly the poor, keep hope and the desire for change alive.

SANDRA CISNEROS

The most acclaimed Chicana author of the early 1990s, Chicago-born Sandra Cisneros began writing at an early age. She has worked as a teacher to high school dropouts, an arts administrator, and a college recruiter, and as a visiting writer in many universities across the country. She is the author of a short novel, The House on Mango Street *(1989), a collection of poetry,* My Wicked, Wicked Ways *(1987), and a collection of short stories,* Woman Hollering Creek *(1991). In the following excerpts from* Little Miracles, Kept Promises, *the author shows the strong faith and devotion to saints that characterize the Mexican-American community in Texas, where she now lives. With a piercing humor and witty style, Cisneros documents the worldly needs and desires of her community, laying bare the economic difficulties and deprivation against which they have to struggle. The author combines personal voices and dreams, religious beliefs, and social criticism in these literary re-creations of votos to the saints.*

Dear San Martín de Porres,
Please send us clothes, furniture, shoes, dishes. We need anything that don't eat. Since the fire we have to start all over again and Lalo's disability check ain't much and don't go far. Zulema would like to finish school but I says she can just forget about it now. She's our oldest and her place is at home helping us out I told her. Please make her see some sense. She's all we got.

Thanking you,
Adelfa Vásquez
Escobas, Texas

Dear San Antonio de Padua,

Can you please help me find a man who isn't a pain in the *nalgas*. There aren't any in Texas, I swear. Especially not in San Antonio.

Can you do something about all the educated Chicanos who have to go to California to find a job. I guess what my sister Irma says is true, "If you didn't get a husband when you were in college, you don't get one."

I would appreciate it very much if you sent a man who speaks Spanish, who at least can pronounce his name the way it's supposed to be pronounced. Someone please who never calls himself "Hispanic" unless he's applying for a grant from Washington, D.C.

Can you send me a man man. I mean someone who's not ashamed to be seen cooking, or cleaning, or looking after himself. In other words, a man who acts like an adult. Not one who's never lived alone, never bought his own under-wear, never ironed his own shirts, never even heated his own tortillas. In other words, don't send me someone like my brothers, who my mother ruined with too much *chichi*, or I'll throw him back.

I'll turn your statue upside down until you send him to me. I've put up with too much too long, and now I'm just too intelligent, too powerful, too beautiful, too sure of who I am finally to deserve anything less.

Ms. Barbara Ybañez
San Antonio, Texas

Seven African Powers that surround our Savior—Obatalia, Yemalia, Ochum, Orula, Ogum, Elegua, and Olofi—why don't you behave and be good to me? Oh Seven African Powers, come on, don't be bad. Let my Illinois lottery ticket

A statue of the Virgin Mary stands among African deities at this makeshift altar where a santeria *ritual is being conducted. An intermingling of Catholicism with religious beliefs brought to the Caribbean through the slave trade,* santeria *is yet another aspect of Latino culture's diversity.*

win, and if it does, don't let my cousin Cirilo in Chicago cheat me out of my winnings, since I'm the one who pays for the ticket and all he does is buy it for me each week—if he does even that. He's my cousin, but like the Bible says, better to say nothing than to say nothing nice.

Protect me from the evil eye of the envious and don't let my enemies do me harm, because I've never done a thing wrong to anyone first. Save this good Christian who the wicked have taken advantage of.

Seven Powers, reward my devotion with good luck. Look after me, why don't you? And don't forget me because I never forget you.

Moises Ildefonso Mata
San Antonio, Texas

Virgencita de Guadalupe,

I promise to walk to your shrine on my knees the very first day I get back, I swear, if you will only get the *Tortillería* La Casa de la Masa to pay me the $253.72 they owe me for two weeks work. I put in 67½ hours that first week and 79 hours the second, and I don't have anything to show for it yet. I calculated with the taxes deducted, I have $253.72 coming to me. That's all I'm asking for. The $253.72 I have coming to me.

I have asked the proprietors Blanquita and Rudy Mondragón, and they keep telling me next week, next week, next week. And it's almost the middle of the third week already and I don't know how I'm going to do it to pay this week's rent, since I'm already behind, and the other guys have loaned me as much as they're able, and I don't know what I'm going to do, I don't know what I'm going to do.

My wife and the kids and my in-laws all depend on what I send home. We are humble people, Virgencita. You know I'm not full of vices. That's how I am. It's been hard for me to live here so far away without seeing my wife, you know. And sometimes one gets tempted, but no, and no, and no. I'm not like that. Please, Virgencita, all I'm asking for is my $253.72. There is no one else I can turn to here in this country, and well, if you can't help me, well, I just don't know.

Arnulfo Contreras
San Antonio, Tejas

Dear San Lázaro,

My mother's comadre Demetria said if I prayed to you that like maybe you could help me because you were raised from the dead and did a lot of miracles and maybe if I lit a candle every night for seven days and prayed, you might maybe could help me with my face breaking out with so many pimples. Thank you.

Ruben Ledesma
Hebbronville, Texas

Saint Jude, patron saint of lost causes,

Help me pass my English 320, British Restoration Literature class and everything to turn out ok.

Eliberto González
Dallas

chichi—breast, refers to breast milk and maternal care
nalgas—butt
tortillería—tortilla factory or store

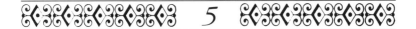

5

OUR WORK

Contrary to stereotypes that characterize them as lazy and unambitious, Latinos and Latinas have contributed enormously to the economy of the United States. For more than a century, Mexicans, Mexican Americans and Central Americans have served in agriculture as field workers, doing manual labor that other Americans refuse. Field-worker families travel from one state to another each season to work for fruit and vegetable growers and to make ends meet. Their children's education often suffers as a result, yet this work cycle defines their lives. Despite the movement to organize these workers during the 1960s and 1970s, headed by César Chávez, low wages and poor working conditions still accompany migrant workers from job to job.

Urban Latinos have tirelessly contributed their work to this nation as well. They have participated in the manufacture of goods, in service positions, and in numerous professions. During World War II, a large influx of Puerto Rican workers in New York City filled factory jobs left by American men who went abroad to fight.

Studies show that, despite all their efforts, Latinos remain among the poorest of the working class in the United States.

*Cesar Chavez (center) also organized workers to protest unsafe farm-
ing methods. In this photo from the mid-1980s, he leads a march
against, as the banner behind him puts it, "La Desgracia de los
Pesticidas"—the disgrace of pesticides.*

NUMBNESS

As immigrant workers, many Latinos and Latinas have taken the poorest-paying jobs under the worst conditions. Because of language barriers, their undocumented status, and cultural differences, many Latinos have not been able to fight for better conditions or higher wages. For those people, work is, at best, a backbreaking, mind-numbing experience that must be endured.

JESÚS COLÓN

A young black cigar-maker from Puerto Rico, Jesús Colón came to New York at the turn of the century as a stowaway in a passenger ship. In "Easy Job, Good Wages," from A Puerto Rican in New York and Other Sketches, *he unveils the physical dangers and hazards that workers are exposed to in factories. Unfortunately, today many of these conditions have not improved.*

This happened early in 1919. We were both out of work, my brother and I. He got up earlier to look for a job. When I woke up, he was already gone. So I dressed, went out and bought a copy of the *New York World* and turned its pages until I got to the "Help Wanted Unskilled" section of the paper. After much reading and re-reading the same columns, my attention was held by a small advertisement. It read: "Easy job. Good wages. No experience necessary." This was followed by a number and street on the West Side of Lower Manhattan. It sounded like the job I was looking for. Easy job. Good wages. Those four words revolved in my brain as I was traveling toward the address indicated in the advertisement. Easy job. Good wages. Easy job. Good wages. Easy . . . .

The place consisted of a small front office and a large loft on the floor of which I noticed a series of large galvanized tubs half filled with water out of which I noticed protruding the necks of many bottles of various sizes and shapes. Around these tubs there were a number of workers, male and female, sitting on small wooden benches. All had their hands in the water of the tub, the left hand holding a bottle and with the thumbnail of the right hand scratching the labels.

The foreman found a vacant stool for me around one of the tubs of water. I asked why a penknife or a small safety razor could not be used instead of the thumbnail to take off the old labels from the bottles. I was expertly informed that knives or razors would scratch the glass thus depreciating the value of the bottles when they were to be sold.

I sat down and started to use my thumbnail on one bottle. The water had somewhat softened the transparent mucilage used to attach the label to the bottle. But the softening did not work out uniformly somehow. There were always pieces of label that for some obscure reason remained affixed to the bottles. It was on those pieces of labels tenaciously fastened to the bottles that my right-hand thumbnail had to work overtime. As the minutes passed I noticed that the coldness of the water started to pass from my hand to my body giving me intermittent body shivers that I tried to conceal with the greatest of effort from those sitting beside me. My hands became deadly clean and tiny little wrinkles started to show especially at the tip of my fingers. Sometimes I stopped a few seconds from scratching the bottles, to open and close my fists in rapid movements in order to bring blood to my hands. But almost as soon as I placed them in the water they became deathly pale again.

But these were minor details compared with what was happening to the thumb of my right hand. From a delicate, boyish thumb, it was growing by the minute into a full-blown tomato-colored finger. It was the only part of my right hand remaining blood red. I started to look at the workers' thumbs. I noticed that these particular fingers on their right hands were unusually developed with a thick layer of corn-like surface at the top of their right thumb. The nails on their thumbs looked coarser and smaller than on the other fingers—thumb and nail having become one and the same thing—a primitive unnatural human instrument especially developed to detach hard pieces of labels from wet bottles immersed in galvanized tubs.

After a couple of hours I had a feeling that my thumbnail was going to leave my finger and jump into the cold water in the tub. A numb pain imperceptibly began to be felt coming from my right thumb. Then I began to feel such pain as if coming from a finger bigger than all of my body.

After three hours of this I decided to quit fast. I told the foreman so, showing him my swollen finger. He figured I had earned 69 cents at 23 cents an hour.

Early in the evening I met my brother in our furnished room. We started to exchange experiences of our job hunting for the day. "You know what?" my brother started. "Early in the morning I went to work where they take labels off old bottles—with your right hand thumbnail. . . . Somewhere on the West Side of Lower Manhattan. I only stayed a couple of hours. 'Easy job. Good wages,' they said. The person who wrote that ad must have had a great sense of humor." And we both had a hearty laugh that evening when I told my brother that I also went to work at that same place later in the day.

Now when I see ads reading, "Easy job. Good wages," I just smile an ancient, tired, knowing smile.

AWAKENING

For many daughters of traditional Latino families, work can be a means of awakening to their potential as individuals, and to a newfound financial independence that allows them greater control over their lives. Some industries in the United States—like the garment industry—have flourished, thanks to overwhelming numbers of Latina women who worked long hours for small wages. But because many factory jobs have moved abroad, these workers have suffered unemployment. The single heads of many households, Latinas have survived by working when jobs are available, and with the support of welfare in times of transition. As a whole, through their active participation in the labor movement, Latinas have overcome double discrimination against them as women and as Latinas.

MARÍA AVILA

María Avila, from New Mexico, dropped out of high school at seventeen, lived on welfare for two years as a single mother, and then became a full-time factory worker. Her active leadership at work as a union steward exemplifies the central role that women of color have played in the labor movement. For Avila, work became a means of political, social, and personal awakening. Her story appears in Las Mujeres: Conversations from a Hispanic Community *(1980).*

꧁꧂ When I was on welfare I wanted to get a job. I hated hanging around the house all day, but I had been shut in so long I was just like a turtle. My sister-in-law lived next door and I used to go over to her house every day, and we didn't have nothing to talk about—just the soap operas. We kept on telling each other we were going to get jobs, but we were both so scared. All she'd ever done was cook and clean house, and I'd just had a couple of part-time waitress jobs. But, finally, one day, we did it. We went down to the unemployment place and we both got jobs working at Lenkhurt. It's an electronics factory, and I work on components. I wind bobbins.

When I got the job at Lenkhurt, it was a real switch. Suddenly I was doing everything, raising a child, working, and taking care of the house. I was doing everything that a man and a woman do when they're in couples, and it felt real good because I didn't have to ask anybody for anything. Then, I started getting to know some of the men at work. Two of them bought me this old car, and now they're teaching me how to fix it up. Things started to change for me. I began to view men differently, and sometimes they saw me differently, too. Before, I'd sort of looked up at them, and now I started to look at them as equals.

The job I've got is a good job, too, considering that I dropped out of high school and I've never had a full-time job before. There are about fifteen hundred people working here. Most of the workers are women and most of the women are Chicanas like me, without much education and with one or two kids to support. You start out making two seventy-six, and then it goes up slowly to three forty-five an hour. The only way you can make more money than that is by incentive or piecework. That's when they give you orders to do, like if you're supposed to do one hundred pieces in an hour and you do two hundred, you get an extra hour's pay. Some of the women here work two hundred percent—that means in eight hours they get sixteen hours' worth of pieces done, and they stick at it. I can't do that. Sometimes I can, but not all the time. It gets to you.

We come into work at seven A.M. and we get off at five. We get a break at nine A.M. for ten minutes, and then we get a half-hour for lunch and a break in the afternoon. But from when you get here, it's rush, rush, rush. And you have to punch in and punch out. They have very strict rules. If you're tardy, they mark it down, kinda like they do in high school.

They mark down your absences, too. You're only allowed to have a certain amount of unexcused absences. Then you have to bring in a slip from the doctor. They give you warnings and then they discipline you if you miss too much. There's a lot of women here who have lost their jobs for being late in the mornings. Like say they have kids, and the nursery didn't open in time, or something like that. That's not considered. A certain amount of absences or tardies and you're out.

We've got a union here now. It's been here for about a year, and it's helped a little bit. We get thirty cents more an hour. From what some of the women say, it's made things worse, though, because before the union, they didn't have such a strict attendance policy. But I think that the company brings these policies in on purpose so that people will think the union's not good for you.

I'm a union steward. I volunteered about a year ago. When the workers have complaints, I go talk to them and I try to settle it with the supervisor, if possible. I also file grievances and things.

There's not very many women in the union. It's mostly men, and I think the women are beginning to see that because they say, "How come those men run the union when we're the ones that work here?" That's why I wanted to be a steward, so we'd have some representation, and the union caucus thought I should try it, too. They made me a steward, but they never gave me any training. If they wanted me so bad, they could have given me some training and prepared me. They have steward meetings, but the meetings only last a half an hour. Everybody just gets together and talks. There's a group of us now that are going to start training ourselves, since the union's not doing it, because we really could do a lot more if we were prepared.

About a year ago some of the guys in the union told me about this Chicano political group they belonged to, and invited me to come to some meetings. The men and women in that group tried really hard to treat each other as equals— even though the men failed a lot, they tried really hard. The women pointed out the way men were ignoring issues like child care. The men really listened. They started taking care of the kids during the meetings. This one couple in the group was invited to go to China, but she got pregnant so he had to go alone. After he got back, though, he got the other end of the deal. She's a photographer and she started working on this book, *450 Years of Chicano Oppression*. So her husband stayed home and took care of the baby while she did the photography.

Most of the men I know are trying to understand the problems between men and women. I've got this one friend, he's a black guy, his name is Alfred Jones. He's nineteen years old, and he's in prison up in Santa Fe. I go up to see him every Saturday, and we talk a lot about equality and the woman question. He's really new to the idea, but he's trying to learn, and he's talking to the other guys in the joint, and asking me for books to read about politics and about women. It makes me really happy to have friends like that.

There's a lot of men, though, who still don't see things my way. Like I'll go out with my friends to dances, and the men will get shocked at the way I act. They say, "Is it all right if I sit with you?" after I've danced with them, and if I tell them no, they're surprised and mad, but if I say yes, they think I like them. So they start holding my hand. I say, "What are you holding my hand for? I'm not a little kid." And they get really burned up and leave. So sometimes it's very hard.

I get along real good with the women at work, though. I can talk to them about more things than the men can, like about the kids and nurseries. When they put in that attendance policy, the women were mad. They said, "Well, if they're going to mark us down when we can't find day care for our kids, we're just going to leave our kids out by the entrance gate. We'll leave them in the guard shack and let the guards deal with them." And so I got to talking to the women about the nurseries they have in China, and how neat it would be to have something like that here. You could go have lunch with your kids, and you could go over to nurse them. So we've got this new demand for our next contract—we want a day-care center at the plant. We may not get it, but we're going to try, because day care is really important to us. And one of these days or years we will get it. I know we will.

Yolanda Lopez describes her painting, The Guadalupe Triptych, *as "a valentine to working women." In the section of the painting shown here, Lopez portrays herself as a symbol of the surging strength of liberated Latinas.*

VISION

Despite the difficult working conditions that Latinos and Latinas have met in the "land of opportunities," many have enhanced their work and their products with their own creativity, originality, and vision.

JUAN FELIPE HERRERA

A Chicano poet, actor, and musician, Juan Felipe Herrera also teaches creative writing to college students and offers writing workshops to prisoners and schoolchildren in California. In his poem "Inside the Jacket," a Mexican tailor, given some freedom by his boss, embroiders a jacket with a magical image that "spreads across the city." Like the jacket, Latino creativity and cultural vision have transformed this country.

I remember, many years ago,
a Mexicano working in a sweatshop
on E Street by the library.

I could see him through the window;
a tailor by trade.

I thought about asking him
to make me a suit for graduation.

His fingers were so thin, so dark.

Usually, he labored on a sport coat.
I could tell the owner had granted him
privacy.

He seemed happy and at ease.
One evening, I passed by and looked
at his finery; his project:

venom lacing
a serpent feverishly winding out of the earth
wrapping around the furniture, into the ceiling,

a gold lacing, swelling
pouring out into the night,
an iridescent skin, leaping
out of his scarred hands,
spreading across the city.

6

LANGUAGE AND OUR IDENTITIES

Latinos and Latinas are as diverse in their language as they are in where they live, their social class, race, and other matters. Many recent immigrants speak only Spanish—but in a wide variety of dialects with differing vocabulary and accents. Their children learn English in school and often serve as translators for them and other relatives. Second- and third-generation Latinos may speak English exclusively.

BANISHED FROM SPANISH

Most Latinos, however, are bilingual, communicating in English and Spanish. Often they can mix both languages in a single sentence or phrase with astounding fluidity and ease, respecting the grammatical rules of each. While many Latino and Latina writers have used this blended speech to forge original and unique writing styles, it has also been dismissed as a sign of ignorance. Schools throughout the country have instituted "English only" policies on the assumption—to many an unfair and prejudiced assumption—that to truly be American one must publicly speak only English. For many Latinos and Latinas, being forced to suppress even the smallest traces of their language means suppressing their identities.

Yet language cannot be legislated. English-influenced Spanish and Spanish-influenced English continue to be spoken as daily life requires. Indeed, many believe that this trade between languages cannot but change the identity of large areas of the United States. By the early 1990s the United States was the fourth-largest Spanish-speaking country in the world and Los Angeles was the second-largest Spanish-speaking city in the hemisphere.

MARTÍN ESPADA

A Puerto Rican poet and lawyer from Massachusetts, Martín Espada equates being banished from Spanish with being dumped on. He was born in Brooklyn, New York, in 1957. This poem, "The New Bathroom Policy at English High School," is excerpted from his collection Rebellion Is the Circle of a Lover's Hands. *His father, Frank Espada, is a well-known photographer.*

The boys chatter Spanish
in the bathroom
while the principal
listens from his stall

The only word he recognizes
is his own name
and this constipates him

So he decides
to ban Spanish
in the bathrooms

Now he can relax

Frank Espada's "Young man with Puerto Rican flag, Washington, D.C., 1981" is from a series the photographer calls The Documentary Project, which records the Puerto Rican experience in the United States and the quest for, among other things, dignidad *(dignity)*.

JOSÉ ANTONIO BURCIAGA

For this Chicano writer, artist, and comedian from Stanford, California, the banning of Spanish in his parochial school in El Paso, Texas, during the 1950s led to feelings of guilt. Yet the author shows us how this "sin" was positively offset by a strong sense of Mexican culture and identity at home. He recalls these memories in "All the Things I Learned in School Weren't Necessarily True," an engaging piece from his book Drink Cultura *that illustrates the effects of "English only" education on young Latinos.*

Perhaps the most memorable experiences one has in school are those that come into direct conflict with one's family's beliefs and traditions. Almost everyone goes through these challenging and unforgettable moments.

My earliest conflict came in kindergarten, when I was given a quiz about nature. "Can the sun shine while it is raining at the same time?" Of course! I had seen it. So I checked off "yes." In El Paso it happened all the time, and forty some years later it still happens. Throughout the Southwest it is a very natural occurrence for many though a phenomenon for others. For Sister Margaret Ann, it was a phenomenon because she had never paid attention.

According to Sister, I was wrong so she put a big, fat, red "X" by my "yes" box. I found it impossible to defend my answer because of the ridicule I received and the anger I felt. In El Paso I can be wincing at the sun and getting wet at the same time. I can drive in and out of flash floods as easy as going from one block to the next.

Four years later, Sister Mary Justin, my fourth-grade teacher told us that God could not do everything. "He can only do what is possible," said Sister Justin. "For instance, God cannot make a circle a square or vice versa or make one plus one equal one."

Well, I didn't believe that for one instant. God could do everything and anything that was good. To change a circle into a square or vice versa was totally plausible. It was a challenge and I eventually solved the impossible divine task so that even a human could change a circle to a square. By making the square out of a piece of string, I could easily transform it into a circle, or could make a squared circle or a circled square. Since then I have also learned that one plus one is not necessarily two and that God is a she and also goes by the name *Quetzalcoatl.*

Then there was Mrs. Roth, our music teacher, who expected all of the sixth-grade class to open their mouths wide to sing and enunciate each syllable to the fullest. The majority of the class was Mexican-American so she decided to tell us that the lines on old Mexican faces were due to the fact that these people didn't open their mouths and enunciate properly when they talked. As sixth graders we weren't ready to hear about age lines on our faces, never mind the fact that we knew those lines were due to old age or a merciless desert sun that engraves character into a face. . . .

But no learning experience was more painful or damaging than the silence imposed on our Mexican culture, history and beautiful Spanish language. To speak Spanish was not only illegal but also a sin: "Bless me Father, for I have sinned. I spoke Spanish in class and during recess. . . ." *Mea culpa, mea culpa, mea máxima culpa!* [The blame is mine, the blame is mine, the greatest blame is mine.] I gently rapped my closed fist on my chest. I knew I would sin again but that was all right because there was always confession, now called "reconciliation."

The silence of our language, culture, and history was broken at home by our Mother, a former schoolteacher in Mexico. She taught her six children to know, love and respect our language, our customs and our history.

And this is one reason why I write—to express those beliefs and to teach what was once a silent sin. These words etched in black ink are made not from individual letters but scars that perforate the paper-like open wounds to the soul of a young Chicano who sought the truth in his own reflection.

Blessed be the teachings of many cultures in the classrooms! Blessed be the truth in her many fashions and forms! Blessed be God in her glory and wisdom!

EXILED TO ENGLISH

What does it mean to a Latino or Latina not to speak Spanish? Often, not possessing the tongue of parents and grandparents becomes a subtle loss of family. It is a slow but constant drift from the past, from roots, from home. Many Latinos who speak only English feel a relentless isolation. Others find the journey away from Spanish an opportunity to discover means of communication that go beyond specific languages and ethnic origins.

LORNA DEE CERVANTES

A Chicana poet from San Jose, California, Lorna Dee Cervantes has been publishing since the 1970s. The speaker of this poem, "Refugee Ship" from the collection Emplumada, *charges her mother with taking away her language, Spanish, probably so that she would fit into American society.*

But the speaker feels like a stranger to herself. Looking in the mirror, she cannot account for her Mexican features. When she says "I'm orphaned from my Spanish name," she may well be pointing to the irony of having the same last name as the most famous author in the Spanish language, Miguel de Cervantes, author of Don Quixote, *yet being unable to speak Spanish.*

Like wet cornstarch, I slide
past my grandmother's eyes. Bible
at her side, she removes her glasses.
The pudding thickens.

Mama raised me without language.
I'm orphaned from my Spanish name.
The words are foreign, stumbling

on my tongue. I see in the mirror
my reflection: bronzed skin, black hair.

I feel I am a captive
aboard the refugee ship.
The ship that will never dock.
El barco que nunca atraca.

el barco que nunca atraca—the ship that never pulls into
dock

RICHARD RODRÍGUEZ

In this excerpt from his much discussed book, Hunger of
Memory, *Mexican-American writer Richard Rodríguez describes the confusion and anguish that accompanied his
move to English as his only language. Spanish had been the
language of intimacy in his family. In losing it, he lost a
sense of closeness with his elders—or so he believed.
Rodríguez goes on to explain that in replacing Spanish with
English he learned that words can only communicate love,
not create it. Thus, human emotions transcend both English
and Spanish.*

I grew up victim to a disabling confusion. As I grew
fluent in English, I no longer could speak Spanish with
confidence. I continued to understand spoken Spanish. And
in high school, I learned how to read and write Spanish. But
for many years I could not pronounce it. A powerful guilt
blocked my spoken words; an essential glue was missing
whenever I'd try to connect words to form sentences. I

would be unable to break a barrier of sound, to speak freely. I would speak, or try to speak, Spanish, and I would manage to utter halting, hiccuping sounds that betrayed my unease.

When relatives and Spanish-speaking friends of my parents came to the house, my brother and sisters seemed reticent to use Spanish, but at least they managed to say a few necessary words before being excused. I never managed so gracefully. I was cursed with guilt. Each time I'd hear myself addressed in Spanish, I would be unable to respond with any success. I'd know the words I wanted to say, but I couldn't manage to say them. I would try to speak, but everything I said seemed to me horribly anglicized. My mouth would not form the words right. My jaw would tremble. After a phrase or two, I'd cough up a warm, silvery sound. And stop.

It surprised my listeners to hear me. They'd lower their heads, better to grasp what I was trying to say. They would repeat their questions in gentle, affectionate voices. But by then I would answer in English. No, no, they would say, we want you to speak to us in Spanish. (". . . *en español.*") But I couldn't do it. *Pocho* then they called me. Sometimes playfully, teasingly, using the tender diminutive—*mi pochito.* Sometimes not so playfully, mockingly, *Pocho.* (A Spanish dictionary defines that word as an adjective meaning "colorless" or "bland." But I heard it as a noun, naming the Mexican-American who, in becoming an American, forgets his native society.) "¡*Pocho!*" the lady in the Mexican food store muttered, shaking her head. I looked up to the counter where red and green peppers were strung like Christmas tree lights and saw the frowning face of the stranger. My mother laughed somewhere behind me. (She said that her children didn't want to practice "our Spanish" after they started going to school.) My mother's smiling voice made me suspect that the lady who faced me was not really angry at me. But, searching her face, I couldn't find the hint of a smile.

Embarrassed, my parents would regularly need to explain their children's inability to speak flowing Spanish during those years. My mother met the wrath of her brother, her only brother, when he came up from Mexico one summer with his family. He saw his nieces and nephews for the very first time. After listening to me, he looked away and said what a disgrace it was that I couldn't speak Spanish, "*su proprio idioma.*" He made that remark to my mother; I noticed, however, that he stared at my father.

I clearly remember one other visitor from those years. A longtime friend of my father from San Francisco would come to stay with us for several days in late August. He took great interest in me after he realized that I couldn't answer his questions in Spanish. He would grab me as I started to leave the kitchen. He would ask me something. Usually he wouldn't bother to wait for my mumbled response. Knowingly, he'd murmur: "*Ay Pocho, Pocho, adónde vas?*" And he would press his thumbs into the upper part of my arms, making me squirm with currents of pain. Dumbly, I'd stand there, waiting for his wife to notice us, for her to call him off with a benign smile. I'd giggle, hoping to deflate the tension between us, pretending that I hadn't seen the glittering scorn in his glance.

I remember that man now, but seek no revenge in this telling. I recount such incidents only because they suggest the fierce power Spanish had for many people I met at home; the way Spanish was associated with closeness. Most of those people who called me a *Pocho* could have spoken English to me. But they would not. They seemed to think that Spanish was the only language we could use, that Spanish alone permitted our close association. (Such persons are vulnerable always to the ghetto merchant and the politician who have learned the value of speaking their clients' family language to gain immediate trust.) For my part, I felt that I had somehow committed a sin of betrayal by learning English. But betrayal against whom? Not against visitors to the house exactly. No, I felt that I had betrayed my immediate family. I *knew* that my parents had encouraged me to learn English. I *knew* that I had turned to English only with angry reluctance. But once I spoke English with ease, I came to *feel* guilty. (This guilt defied logic.) I felt that I had shattered the intimate bond that had once held the family close. This original sin against my family told whenever anyone addressed me in Spanish and I responded, confounded.

But even during those years of guilt, I was coming to sense certain consoling truths about language and intimacy. I remember playing with a friend in the backyard one day, when my grandmother appeared at the window. Her face was stern with suspicion when she saw the boy (the *gringo*) I was with. In Spanish she called out to me, sounding the whistle of her ancient breath. My companion looked up and watched her intently as she lowered the window and moved, still visible, behind the light curtain, watching us both. He wanted to know what she had said. I started to tell him, to say—to translate her Spanish words into English. The problem was, however, that though I knew how to translate exactly *what* she had told me, I realized that any translation would distort the deepest meaning of her message: It had been directed only to me. This message of intimacy could never be translated because it was not *in* the words she had used but passed *through* them. So any translation would have seemed wrong; her words would have been stripped of an essential meaning. Finally, I decided not to tell my friend anything. I told him that I didn't hear all she had said.

This insight unfolded in time. Making more and more friends outside my house, I began to distinguish intimate voices speaking through *English*. I'd listen at times to a close friend's confidential tone or secretive whisper. Even more remarkable were those instances when, for no special reason apparently, I'd become conscious of the fact that my companion was speaking only to me. I'd marvel just hearing his voice. It was a stunning event: to be able to break through his words, to be able to hear this voice of the other, to realize that it was directed only to me. After such moments of intimacy outside the house, I began to trust hearing intimacy conveyed through my family's English. Voices at home at last punctured sad confusion. I'd hear myself addressed as an intimate at home once again. Such moments were never as raucous with sound as past times had been when we had had "private" Spanish to use. (Our English-sounding house was never to be as noisy as our Spanish-speaking house had been.) Intimate moments were usually soft moments of sound. My mother was in the dining room while I did my homework nearby. And she looked over at me. Smiled. Said something—her words said nothing very important. But her voice sounded to tell me (*We are together*) I was her son.

(*Richard!*)

Advertisements in "a crowded city of words," Miami, Florida. The bilingualism of many Latinos is reflected everywhere in this and other American cities, such as New York and Los Angeles.

Intimacy thus continued at home; intimacy was not stilled by English. It is true that I would never forget the great change of my life, the diminished occasions of intimacy. But there would also be times when I sensed the deepest truth about language and intimacy: *Intimacy is not created by a particular language; it is created by intimates.* The great change in my life was not linguistic but social. If, after becoming a successful student, I no longer heard intimate voices as often as I had earlier, it was not because I spoke English rather than Spanish. It was because I used public language for most of the day. I moved easily at last, a citizen in a crowded city of words.

"Ay, Pocho, Pocho, adónde vas?"—"Oh, Pocho, Pocho, where are you going?"
"su proprio [*sic*] *idioma"*—"his own language"

7

RACE AND RACIAL DISCRIMINATION

Among the many consequences of the Spanish Conquest of this hemisphere was *mestizaje. Mestizaje* refers to the mixture of races that characterizes all Latinos. During the more than five hundred years since Columbus stumbled onto Watling Island in the Caribbean, Europeans have come to this hemisphere and had children with Indian people. Captive Africans have also had children with Europeans, Indians, and their mixed offspring. As a result, Latinos are among the most racially diverse people in the world.

RACE

Since we are all the sons and daughters of *mestizaje,* Latinos and Latinas have tended to maintain tolerant and open attitudes toward racial difference. Siblings in the same Latino family often range from having light skin and European features to dark, bronze, or black with African features. Yet notions of a connection between skin color and racial superiority—instilled mostly by the Spanish during the years they colonized vast portions of Central and Latin

115

This drawing, El Mestizo, *by César A. Martínez, symbolizes* mestizaje. *The Spanish bull, representing Europe, and the American jaguar coalesce into the young Latino artist at the center.*

America—persist. Within Latino families, darker-skinned children can become the victims of prejudice and exclusion—sometimes even by their own parents.

GLORIA ANZALDÚA

A Chicana writer from Texas, Gloria Anzaldúa is the author of Borderlands—La Frontera. *She has also edited important collections of writings on women of color, including* This Bridge Called My Back. *From that volume comes this excerpt of "La Prieta" ("The Dark-Skinned Woman"), an essay in which Anzaldúa writes about how her family internalized racial stereotypes and how they affected her own sense of herself as a woman.*

When I was born, *Mamágrande* Locha inspected my buttocks looking for the dark blotch, the sign of *indio,* or worse, of mulatto blood. My grandmother (Spanish, part German, the hint of royalty lying just beneath the surface of her fair skin, blue eyes and the coils of her once blond hair) would brag that her family was one of the first to settle in the range country of south Texas.

Too bad *mihijita* was *morena, muy prieta,* so dark and different from her own fair-skinned children. But she loved mihijita anyway. What I lacked in whiteness, I had in smartness. But it *was* too bad I was dark like an Indian.

"Don't go out in the sun," my mother would tell me when I wanted to play outside. "If you get any darker, they'll mistake you for an Indian. And don't get dirt on your clothes. You don't want people to say you're a dirty Mexican." It never dawned on her that, though sixth-generation American, we were still Mexican and that all Mexicans are part Indian. I passed my adolescence combating her incessant orders to bathe my body, scrub the floors and cupboards, clean the windows and the walls.

And as we'd get into the back of the "patron's" truck that would take us to the fields, she'd ask, "Where's your *gorra* [sunbonnet]?" *La gorra*—rim held firm by slats of cardboard, neck flounce flowing over my shoulders—made me feel like a horse with blinders, a member of the French Foreign Legion, or a nun bowed down by her wimple.

One day in the middle of the cotton field, I threw the *gorra* away and donned a sombrero. Though it didn't keep out the Texas 110° sun as well as the bonnet, I could now see in all directions, feel the breeze, dry the sweat on my neck.

When I began writing this essay, nearly two years ago, the wind I was accustomed to suddenly turned into a hurricane. It opened the door to the old images that haunt me, the old ghosts and all the old wounds. Each image a sword that cuts through me, each word a test. Terrified, I shelved the rough draft of this essay for a year.

I was terrified because in this writing I must be hard on people of color who are the oppressed victims. I am still afraid because I will have to call us on a lot of shit like our own racism, our fear of women and sexuality. One of my biggest fears is that of betraying myself, of consuming myself with self-castigation, of not being able to unseat the guilt that has ridden on my back for years.

> These my two hands
> quick to slap my face
> before others could slap it

From my poem "The Woman Who Lived Forever."

But above all, I am terrified of making my mother the villain in my life rather than showing how she has been a victim. Will I be betraying her in this essay for her early disloyalty to me?

indio—Indian
Mamágrande—literally Big Mother, refers to grandmother
mihijita—my dear daughter
morena—a dark-skinned woman
muy prieta—very dark

RACIAL DISCRIMINATION

While issues of race have divided Latinos among themselves, racial discrimination against Latinos by government institutions and authorities has divided them from society. Like African Americans, Latinos, particularly in inner cities, have been systematically abused and oppressed—often by police—because of their skin color and accents.

LUIS J. RODRIGUEZ

A Chicano writer from East Los Angeles, Luis Rodriguez is the author of the highly acclaimed Always Running, La Vida Loca: Gang Days in Los Angeles, *an account of his experiences as a gang member in East L.A. He has also published collections of poems, among them* The Concrete River, *from which this poem, "The Best of Us," comes. Rodriguez offers a moving account of how discrimination can alter forever many lives in a matter of minutes. The poem also offers hope for the future, but only if communities organize to end discrimination against Latinos and indeed all people.*

Epitaphs hang like clothes on a line.
They are smeared with a whitewash,
the color of injustice.
Hypocritical prayers fill the sweat of days,
flowing down the empty lots and alleys
where my boy plays.
Denial clings to my skin;
a breathy wind keeps bringing it back.
They say I should be glad I do not hunger,
but I'm starving with the pangs of discontent.
The nightmares never cease:
A shackled corpse on blood-soaked sheets.
The .357 magnum's smoking nostril at my belly.
A shadowed face screaming for reprisals.
A child with unknowing eyes asking for his father.

Birdlike, I hover above the grave,
quivering on broken wings.
Inside is a statue of clay,
your body,
made-over with a mouth clenched in silence.
I wait for the moment when you rise.
I want to pour over you this aborted love,
draining from me along with tears.
You never do awaken.
You never provide a hint of recognition.
They say it's God's will. They say I must go on.
I do—carrying you with me.
But every path stops with you.
Every beginning is you.
If not for this seed growing to manhood,
a seed you never see change into its seasons,
I would fail to meet every dawn.

Even now I try to disembark.
But everything—
the wind on my face,
the sparkle of stars at night,
the blast of sun on my back—
is as it was when you tenderly fashioned
my body beneath you.

"Ladies and gentlemen of the jury: The prosecution will show how the plaintiff in this case gave birth to a son, who is the true child of the deceased. And how his untimely death has deprived this infant boy of knowing his father, or the love, care, and attention he could have provided, if . . . ."

Transcript machines clicking.
Witnesses, looking like sad paintings,
sit in pews of swirled wood.
Policemen laugh in the hallways.
For months I visit these marbled corridors,
push myself through sterilized aisles
and think of facing the jury,
of tearing my eyes out of their sockets,
and saying: "Take these—see what I have seen!"
The lies come dressed in suits and ties;
they lurk behind badges and smothered grins.
Take these eyes and know the truth.
Instead, I'm drowning in a sea of legal terms,
forensic jargon—policies and procedures.
More lies.

When it's my turn to testify, I stutter.
It's a voice of lessened humanity.
A woman's bitter musings
through a veil of solitude.

A plea crawling from the curbside.
They have my name and thereby possess me.
I am that *chola*,
that street-girl buried in the crazy life.
I did not commit any crime.
But I am a woman of dark skin
and a darker heritage.
This is my crime.

"Will you tell the truth, the whole truth, and nothing but the truth, so help you God?

"I will."

"State your name and address for the record please."

"My name is Delia Torres . . . but everyone calls me Dee Dee. I live on 1132 Hazard Avenue, East Los Angeles."

"Okay, Delia—Dee Dee—will you please tell the jury what happened the night of March 15, 1981 . . . and please be as explicit as you can. You understand explicit, don't you?"

"Yes sir, I mean, I know what you mean . . . sir—"

" 'Yes' is a good enough answer, thank you. Now tell us, in your own words, what happened?"

What I couldn't tell:
The way the night seemed to sing into being
on a day full of the lust of spring.
The way your mom carefully emptied
a pot of water that had been soaking with beans.
How your brother Tony sat in front of the TV,
its greenish-blue lights changing tints
across his face.
This was my first dinner with your family.

Alone, pregnant, I finally felt enveloped
in firm arms.
A former ward of the state, abandoned,
I had to scrape a life out of narrow streets . . .
until your family took me in.
They made me believe there could be something
like home, like love,
something I could wake up to and touch—
that it was not an illusion.
Your mother made a funny remark
and something alien—laughter—burst forth
from me,
like a butterfly out of a cocoon
woven from warmth inside.
And everyone, including your dad,
lying in bed then
with a broken thigh bone from a work injury,
accepted me,
made me want to be your wife,
the mother of your child.
Remember how you smiled that day . . .
how you and your brother
playfully pushed each other and I said,
"Don't make me come in and belt you guys."

"Walter Joseph Coles, 14 years as an officer of the Los Angeles County Sheriff's Department. Numerous citations for brave conduct. A father of three boys. On March 15, 1981, Deputy Coles shot and killed one, Guillermo "Memo" Tovar, 17 years old, and injured one, Antonio "Tony" Tovar, 19 years old. Said suspects were believed to be endangering the life of Deputy Coles at the time of the incident. The sheriff's office

interdepartmental review finds this to be a case of justifiable
homicide due to circumstances of possible injury or death to
said officer.

Following routine paid suspension, Deputy Coles has
been reinstated and transferred to another subdivision of
the county."

Oh, I want to scream out my lungs!
The things they say about you!
How you were once caught joyriding,
that you were a gang member.
A delinquent.
But that's not you!
You were Memo,
a handsome *prieto* with a face
that could have been carved
from the darkest mahogany.
Memo, with sharp brown eyes
that pierced the placid smiles
and phony demeanors the rest of us wore as masks.
You played football, baseball—ran track.
You planned to get good grades
and go to college . . . to be somebody decent.
Remember the time we walked home from school
and you spotted a tall hedge of ivy.
Remember. You tossed up a challenge.
"You think I can jump over it?"
The hedge was high and bushy.
I said no.
But you moved back, bent low
and took in the distance.
Then you got on your hands,
paused there on the sidewalk,

and suddenly leaped forward—running fast,
like an Olympic athlete,
like an Indian over rocky streams.
When you jumped, it was so smooth
you could have been a kite of bright colors,
sailing on a low wind,
and me holding the string.
You made it over. You always made it over.
Memo, you were the best of us.

"Mr. Coles, isn't it a fact that you've had a track record of abuse, beatings, and uncontrolled violent tempers—"

"No, this is totally unfounded."

"Then why is there a record of numerous complaints of unwarranted arrests and shootings in those communities, black and Mexican, in which you have served in the capacity of a peace officer in the County of Los Angeles?"

"Those are unsubstantiated claims."

"Now, Mr. Coles, they can't all be wrong."

"I object, your honor—"

"Objection sustained. . . . Please continue another line of questioning, counsel."

"Okay then, isn't it true, Mr. Coles, that the willful and unlawful murder of this boy, and the maiming of his brother, are acts that culminated a career-long pattern of brutality?"

"No, it's not. I stand on a record of exceptional conduct."

You can't know.
After the shootings,
you were taken to the prison ward
of the County Hospital.

They put leather straps on your arms and legs
but you couldn't move anyway.
They put tubes through your mouth
that couldn't speak anyway.
Your father and mother were also handcuffed,
even with the cast on your dad's leg.
You can't know how all your friends—
Danny Boy, Filo, Serafin—were arrested
and booked for your murder!
Because they happened to be there!
And your brother Tony, shot in the head,
but still alive. His ear gone.
You can't know how mangled your body looked;
bruised and caked with a kind of black paste
they said was your blood.

*"Ms. Torres, we know this is difficult for you . . . but please
try to compose yourself. Now, tell the court what you saw, as
you experienced it, that night of the shootings. . . . Take your
time . . . Ms. Torres, Ms. Torres . . . Your honor, I think she's
fainted."*

I try and try to understand it.
To know where the night failed us.
But I can't. We did nothing wrong.
It started out as a beautiful day.
That afternoon Danny Boy, Filo, and Serafin
came over with a case of beer:
Talking the day away.
Then they drove by, slow,
in a black and white vehicle—
Deputy Coles and Deputy Daryl Tatum:
An Anglo cop and a black cop.

Coles got out of the car and started shouting.
I ran to the window and looked outside.
All of you were spread-eagled
with your hands across the car's hood.
"What's going on, Dee Dee?" your mother asked.
"I don't know. It's cops," I answered.
"They got Memo and the boys."
Then Tony got up.
"What? They got Memo!"
Before I knew it he ran out.
I looked out the window
and saw Tony run up to the officers.
There was arguing.
Danny Boy said something,
I don't know what, but I saw Coles
strike him in the belly with his flashlight.
You turned around and Tatum pushed you back.
Then for no reason at all,
Coles turned to Tony and started calling him
all kinds of names.
From then on everything seemed like a dream.
Tony ran. Coles dashed after him.
Tatum pulled out a gun and held it over you
and the other guys.
Tony rushed into the house but Coles
tackled him in the living room.
A lamp crashed to the floor.
Your mother screamed.
I could hear your dad shout from the bedroom,
"What's going on in there?"
I backed into the kitchen,
next to your mom—

Life and death among poor urban Latinos are dramatized in this detail from the painting, Getting Them Out of the Car, *by John Valdez. Referring to the class and racial discrimination that often result in violence against Chicanos, Valdez writes: "In downtown L.A., death is environmental and economic."*

instinctively placing a hand
over my womb.
Then Coles, standing over Tony,
who lay there on the floor,
got out his gun from a black leather holster.
And I heard your mother shout, "No, not *mijo*, no!"
But he fired it. He fired at Tony's head,
him lying there.
I screamed, and then you burst in.
You came in yelling as you jumped on Coles' back.
Coles fell forward.
Then he grappled with you.
Somehow he pushed you off
and you landed on the sofa.
But Coles didn't hesitate.
He had the gun ready, cocked.
It went off again in a flash of fire.
You fell back, holding your belly, groaning.
Your dad crawled into the living room
and saw you sink into the sofa.
Deputy Tatum ran into the house
just then and looked at everything:
the blood, the broken lamp, the bodies . . .
your fainted mother on the kitchen floor—
Deputy Coles with his gun pointed at me.
I stood silent, like I wasn't there,
frozen by a sound shrouded in terror.
Paralyzed, my arms don't move, my feet don't move,
my brain on hold, unable to talk;
only the beating of a heart continued.
Deputy Tatum dropped his arm
that had been holding a gun.

In a muffled tenor,
breaking the quiet that was beginning
to strangle me,
he said, "Oh my God, oh my God . . . ."

*"Will the foreman please step forward. Has the jury reached
a verdict?*

"Yes, we have, your honor."

"And what is that verdict, please?"

*"We find the defendant, Walter J. Coles, not guilty as
charged."*

Do you know about boys, Mister Coles?
Do you know about what it takes
to see their faces
hide in the pain
of growing into men?

*"Miss Torres, we feel you must know the progress of your son,
Guillermo, Jr. He is very much into himself. Other kids try to
play with him, but he just sits in a corner, alone. Now, he is a
very intelligent boy, and extremely helpful for a three-year-
old. For example, Guillermo likes to pick up chairs and toys
after everyone is through for the day. But he doesn't partici-
pate in the games we play as a group. Now . . . we don't want
to force him, but we feel you must know about this situation
so we can work together in bringing him out. Miss Torres,
can you please tell us what, if anything, may be bothering
him. . . ."*

Everything began to crumble then.
Tony never did get over it;
the anger gnawing at him, day after day.

He's in jail now, but you know that.
Your father stopped working.
It was as if he stopped living too.
His lifelong belief in this country,
its promises, betrayed.
Why then did he sweat and labor all his life?
Why did he fight overseas,
carrying the American flag on a hill in Korea?
Your mom, bless her, keeps the house going,
cleaning every day and seeing that the crumbling
won't cave in on her.
Oh we took the case to civil court, sure,
filing an unlawful death suit.
But the time passed on, our money went dry,
and there is only $4,000 in reparations.
I wish something would shatter my skull
and this memory. I'm wrong, I know,
but how does one be right about this?
Tell me, Memo?
How can I find the courage—
to stop waking up night after night,
to stop this crying into wilted flowers?
Our son keeps growing.
What answers do I give him?
How do I explain?
"Well, *mijito*, your daddy had his guts blown out
by a racist cop and $4,000 is supposed to make it better."

*"We have come together here to demand justice. So many of
our sons have been killed. So many of our fathers . . . this
must stop now! The community has to pool its resources—
crossing barrio lines, language lines—and demand an end*

*to this armed camp called East Los Angeles. The police have
the power of life and death here. We must take this power
from them. . . . Take our destiny into our hands, to forge a
community worthy of its residents; one which will benefit all
of us—documented or undocumented, young or old, man
or woman. . . . Memo Tovar still lives—in our memory and
in our struggle. . . . ¡Ya Basta! No more police murders!"*

We almost left the neighborhood.
We almost had to.
Cops harassed us every day,
watching us come and go.
But people rallied around us,
helping take care of your mom
and dad, the boy and me.
Others have been beaten,
killed.
So there have been protests, marches.
They are gathering again today,
and I will march with them.
They are organizing an anti-police abuse group,
and I will be at the meetings.
The community has stepped into your shoes—
to protect your interests now that you can't.
I have hope for our child—
and for all the children here and everywhere
whose mothers have known the sorrow
of withered breasts,
but also the joy of watching
these cords of humanity
blossom in the sun.
I got a job—finally!—

and your boy is in day care,
doing so much better!
Oh, smile for me, Memo,
smile and break apart
the crystal walls of your death
surrounding us.
Climb out of this hole,
trample the flowers,
be this dream,
this man.
My Memo . . . .

Sources

Rafael Chacón selection from *Legacy of Honor: The Life of Rafael Chacón, a Nineteenth-Century New Mexican*, edited by Jacqueline Dorgan Meketa. Albuquerque: University of New Mexico Press, 1986. Reprinted by permission of the publisher.

"Snaps of Immigration" first appeared in *Red Beans* by Victor Hernández Cruz, Coffee House Press, 1991. Reprinted by permission of the publisher. Copyright © 1991 by Victor Hernández Cruz.

Julia Alvarez selection from *How the Garcia Girls Lost Their Accents*. Copyright © 1991 by Julia Alvarez. Published by Plume, an imprint of New American Library, a division of Penguin Books, USA, Inc. Originally published in hardcover by Algonquin Books of Chapel Hill. Reprinted by permission of Susan Bergholz Literary Services.

"Roots: A Crosscultural Context" by David Unger from *Hispanic Immigrant Writers and the Question of Identity*. Jackson Heights, NY: Ollantay Press, 1989. Reprinted by permission of the publisher.

"La Migra" by Ramón "Tianguis" Pérez is reprinted with permission from the publisher of *Diary of an Undocumented Immigrant*. Houston: Arte Publico Press–University of Houston, 1991.

"Along the Rio Santa Cruz" by Margarita Martínez from *Images and Conversations: Mexican Americans Recall a Southwestern Past*, edited by Patricia Preciado Martin. Tucson: University of Arizona Press, 1988. Reprinted by permission of the publisher.

"The Rhythms" by Willie Colón. Copyright © 1988 by Willie Colón. Reprinted by permission of the author.

Further Reading

Algarín, Miguel, and Miguel Piñeiro, eds. *Nuyorican Poetry: An Anthology of Puerto Rican Words and Feelings.* New York: Morrow, 1975.

Alurista. *Floricanto en Aztlán.* Los Angeles: UCLA Chicano Studies Center Publications, 1971.

Alvarez, Julia. *Homecoming.* New York: Grove Press, 1984.

Antush, John V. *Recent Puerto Rican Theater: Five Plays from New York.* Houston: Arte Público Press, 1991.

Augenbraum, Harold, and Ivan Stavans, eds. *Growing Up Latino: Memoirs and Stories.* New York and Boston: Houghton Mifflin, 1993.

Chávez, Denise. *The Last of the Menu Girls.* Houston: Arte Público Press, 1986.

Chávez, Denise, and Linda Feyder, eds. *Shattering the Myth: Plays by Hispanic Women.* Houston: Arte Público Press, 1992.

Cofer, Judith Ortiz. *Terms of Survival.* Houston: Arte Público Press, 1987.

Duran, Roberto, Judith Ortiz Cofer, and Gustavo Perez Firmat. *Triple Crown.* Tempe, Ariz.: Bilingual Press, 1987.

138

Esteves, Sandra María. *Bluestown Mockingbird Mambo*. Houston: Arte Público Press, 1990.

García, Cristina. *Dreaming in Cuban*. New York: Knopf, 1992.

Gonzalez, Ray, ed. *After Aztlán: Latino Poets of the Nineties*. Boston: Godine, 1992.

————. *Mirrors Beneath the Earth: Short Fiction by Chicano Writers*. Willimantic, CT: Curbstone Press, 1992.

Hollander, Kurt, ed. *The Portable Lower East Side: Latinos in New York City*. Vol. 5, nos. 1 and 2, 1988.

Laviera, Tato. *Enclave*. Houston: Arte Público Press, 1985.

————. *Mainstream Ethics*. Houston: Arte Público Press, 1988.

Mohr, Nicholasa. *El Bronx Remembered*. Houston: Arte Público Press, 1986.

————. *Nilda*. Houston: Arte Público Press, 1986.

————. *Rituals of Survival: A Woman's Portfolio*. Houston: Arte Público Press, 1986.

Muñoz, Elías Miguel. *Crazy Love*. Houston: Arte Público Press, 1989.

Pietri, Pedro. *Puerto Rican Obituary*. New York: Monthly Review Press, 1973.

Poey, Delia, and Virgil Suarez, eds. *Iguana Dreams: New Latino Fiction*. New York: HarperCollins, 1992.

Ponce, Mary Helen. *The Wedding*. Houston: Arte Público Press, 1989.

Soto, Gary. *Living Up the Street: Narrative Recollections*. San Francisco: Strawberry Hill Press, 1985.

————. *Pacific Crossing*. New York and London: Harcourt Brace Jovanovich, 1992.

Suarez, Virgil. *The Cutter*. New York: Ballantine, 1991.

Villanueva, Tino. *Shaking Off the Dark*. Houston: Arte Público Press, 1984.

Index

About the Editor

Frances R. Aparicio is Associate Professor of Romance Languages and Literature and of American Culture at the University of Michigan, Ann Arbor.

She is a specialist in the field of Latino literature in the United States. On this subject she has edited two books, contributed to four volumes of essays, and given some thirty lectures around the world.